The Hell
Jesus
Never Intended

KEITH WRIGHT

THE HELL

JESUS
NEVER
INTENDED

Northstone

Editors: James Taylor, Michael Schwartzentruber
Cover and interior design: Margaret Kyle
Cover art work: Public Domain and Getty Images
Proofreader: Dianne Greenslade

Unless otherwise noted, all biblical quotations come from the New Revised Standard Version of the Bible, copyright 1989 by the Division of Christian Education of the National Council of Churches of Christ in the United States of America, and are used by permission.

The sources of other quotations are identified in the Endnotes. Wherever these quotations use exclusively masculine pronouns or references, they have been quoted as originally published, although the author prefers to use inclusive references that do not attribute specific genders to either God or humans in general.

Northstone Publishing is an imprint of Wood Lake Books, Inc. Wood Lake Books acknowledges the financial support of the Government of Canada, through the Book Publishing Industry Development Program (BPIDP) for its publishing activities.

Wood Lake Books is an employee-owned company, committed to caring for the environment and all creation. Wood Lake Books recycles, reuses, and encourages readers to do the same. Resources are printed on recycled paper and more environmentally friendly groundwood papers (newsprint), whenever possible. The trees used are replaced through donations to the Scoutrees For Canada Program. A percentage of all profit is donated to charitable organizations.

Library and Archives Canada Cataloguing in Publication
Wright, Keith, 1931–
      The Hell Jesus never intended/Keith Wright.
Includes index.
ISBN 1-896836-65-8
1.Hell – Christianity. 2.Church and social problems. I.Title.
BT837.W74 2004   236'.25   C2004-904618-7

Published by Northstone Publishing
an imprint of WOOD LAKE BOOKS, INC.
9025 Jim Bailey Road, Kelowna, BC, Canada, V4V 1R2
250.766.2778
www.northstone.com

Printing 10 9 8 7 6 5 4 3 2 1

Printed in Canada by Transcontinental

DEDICATION

To my wife, Mona, whose musical talents have enriched my life
and my ministry for over 50 years. She taught me that
one approach to Divine Truth and an encounter with God
can be found through music which speaks both to
the heart and to the mind. For this insight I am deeply
grateful.

TABLE OF CONTENTS

FOREWORD

Words have power. Christians, it seems, have always known this. At the center of our faith is the claim of the Word made flesh, the Word endowed with God's power, the Word who incarnates God's love and redeems creation. The words we use in response to that Word expressing what God is doing in Jesus Christ *matter*; they can distort the Good News as well as proclaim it.

Especially, words about Hell. Words about Hell convey enormous power. The fires of Hell have captured the terror, imagination, and passion of Christians across two millennia, and those fires continue to rage today.

In our day, the rhetoric of Hell tends to fall in one of two directions: On the one hand are many who depict Hell's fire with reckless abandon and construe the Good News as salvation *from* eternal damnation. Whether these descriptions come in the form of tractates, fire-and-brimstone preaching, or the zeal of Christian mission, the power of these words is obvious, kindling fearful consequences of a life lived apart from God's love. At the same time, though, these words reduce the Gospel to a reward and punishment schema — good news for those who fear, bad news for those who do not.

On the other hand are Christians who have become embarrassed by the self-righteous rhetoric of Hell, who consider the concept of damnation a theological anachronism antithetical to a God of love. Fearful of distorting Christ's Good News, many Christians avoid talking about Hell altogether. At times, this absence of words can result in a gospel of cheap comfort that is unable to address the hellish conditions of life on our war-ravaged, famine-ridden, ecologically threatened planet.

In this thought-provoking book, Keith Wright offers a clear alternative to reckless words about Hell that terrorize and an absence of words that avoid the often hellish nature of human life. Through a careful analysis of biblical texts, theological trajectories, and pastoral situations, Wright offers welcome words on a topic that has proved embarrassing and horrifying for far too long.

At the center of his work is a rejection of Hell as eternal punishment that awaits the unrighteous and a reclamation of Hell as a reality that we create for ourselves and others in the present. The Good News is not that we are saved *from* fires that loom in the future, but that God frees us *for* abundant life with each other, with creation, and with God's very self for all time. Jesus Christ doesn't save us *from* Hell, but saves us *for* God and each other. The result of this accessibly written account is a theology that opens our eyes again to the bedazzling diversity of creation – the creation that God beholds in the beginning as "very good" and wills to redeem in the end. Keith Wright names the Hell of the future as a distortion of Jesus' message and ministry. He turns our attention to the relentless, ever-surprising love of God that embraces all creation and empowers us to live into God's future. Facing the hells of our time – war, addiction, racism, famine, religious intolerance, and ecological destruction – we recognize that they do not offer the final word, but that God includes us as participants in God's Reign. And that is a word of tremendous power.

David H. Jensen
Assistant Professor of Reformed Theology
Austin Presbyterian Theological Seminary

PREFACE

After reading the manuscript of this book, a friend asked to whom I was writing. My quick answer was, "to everyone." It was too easy an answer. Because when I thought more about it, his question forced me to realize that there are actually three specific and distinct groups of people that I want to address.

The first group is those who believe in a literal, fiery Hell to which God consigns some people after death. I realize that I have been greatly influenced by living in the Southern Bible Belt of the United States. In Texas where I live, people still go door-to-door handing out pamphlets which warn that those who do not accept the sacrifice of Christ on the Cross will surely go to Hell. There is a fundamentalist, literalist bent to the area in which I was raised and where I served in the ministry for over 40 years. I have heard people talk about how, as a child, they were afraid that they might die before they were baptized and thus end up in Hell. When I served as a hospital chaplain one summer, I remember discussions about whether a Protestant minister could baptize a Roman Catholic baby that wasn't expected to live in order to save it from Limbo, a lesser form of Hell to which babies who have not yet been baptized are consigned.

I realize that my experience has colored my thinking. I have seen the fear that Hell instills in people. I have also seen the divisiveness of this doctrine of Hell which not only pits Christians against all other religions but which often pits one group of Christians against another group of Christians. I have seen a family member rejected because she joined a denomination that the family felt would lead her to Hell.

I am aware of the fact that what I have written will challenge some of the core beliefs of those who believe firmly in an eternal, fiery Hell. If you are a part of this group, I can only hope that you will take the challenge to read on.

Let me try to entice you to read further by sharing a story with you.

Recently, I was talking with a friend who said that his Sunday school class had raised the question: "How many people would end up in Hell?" I told him that I did not believe in Hell as an eternal punishment imposed upon people by God. I knew that my friend had a son who had been on drugs and whose life had been greatly damaged by his addiction and by those with whom he associated. The son, who was now a grown man, still lived at home because he found it difficult to stay drug-free and keep a job.

I asked my friend, his father, if he could ever consign his son to live eternally in a pit of fire. He immediately said, "No."

I then asked him if that meant that he was more compassionate than the God he thought was going to send people to Hell for not believing in Jesus Christ. He said he would think about that point. I hope you will, too.

The second group is those who have long ago dismissed the concept of Hell as being too repulsive an idea to attribute to God. If a father or mother would not consign their child to awful pain and suffering forever, how could we possibly believe that God would do so? These people have simply rejected the idea of Hell.

However, what if God doesn't send us to Hell, but we ourselves choose to live in the Hell of fear or anger or self-loathing or meaninglessness or despair? What if we choose to devote ourselves to the acquisition of things and end up lonely and empty because we were so busy we never developed deep relationships in the family or among friends? What if others create conditions that make life hellish for us – war, poverty, injustice, tyranny, slave labor, prostitution, child or sexual abuse – and we do not have enough power to change our situation?

Indeed, what if God, rather than sending people to Hell, is working to get people out of the Hell that they or society have produced? What if Hell is not a place of future punishment but rather a present reality from which God seeks to rescue us by the power of love and acceptance and by showing us the way to life that is full and free? What if we can recapture the meaning of Hell without going back to the old, traditional concept of Hell? If you think that is possible, read on.

Finally, I want to address what I believe is a vast group of people in the middle – those who have grown up in the church and who don't know what to believe about Hell. Many Christians today hear very little about Hell from the pulpit. But they still use words about Hell – in their liturgy, hymns, and in the theology of the church, which refers to salvation and to the claim that it is solely through Jesus Christ that people can be cleansed of their sins and thus made acceptable to God. We talk about God's great love for all people. We teach our children to sing, "Jesus loves me, this I know, for the Bible tells me so." But lingering behind all this talk of God's love is an assumption that we are unlovable sinners who can approach God *only* through the sacrifice of Jesus that satisfies the justice of God and makes us worthy to be in the Divine presence. If this be true, then what happens to all those people who don't believe in Jesus Christ? Do they go to Hell? And what does it mean to believe in Jesus Christ? In Jesus' description of the last judgment, commonly called the Parable of the Sheep and the Goats, he doesn't say anything about believing in him as the key to our future destination. He says that those who have cared for people in need will enter into God's kingdom, and that eternal punishment awaits those who did *not* care for the sick, did not provide for people in need of clothes and shelter, did not provide food and water for people who were hungry or thirsty.

Could that kingdom of God that Jesus talks about be a present reality that we enter in this life when we create the conditions that lead to happiness and peace, and could the punishment to which he refers point to the kind of present Hell that we experience when we fail to love and serve one another?

Clergy and teachers have not done a very good job of helping members wrestle with the concept of salvation and its implications for Heaven and Hell. I am convinced that laypeople are capable of understanding the historical development of the concept of Heaven and Hell and of seeing how Jesus' statements about Hell fit into that historical context. I am also convinced that lay people need a theological overview of the many different understandings of what God was doing in Christ's death on the Cross in order to challenge the most prevalent pronouncements about salvation.

If you are a part of this large third group of people who feel uneasy about the idea of Hell as eternal punishment but have never been given the historical or theological tools to challenge it, I invite you to read on. But remember that this is not just an intellectual adventure. If I am right in what I write, I will be equipping you, and hopefully the clergy who guide you, to challenge the exclusivity of the Christian faith which has often claimed to have the only way to escape Hell. I will be giving you the rationale to refocus our attention on Hell as a present reality rather than a place of eternal punishment. The results will certainly be worth the effort if we can offer the world a more biblically accurate picture of God's intention to save us from Hell in this life and if we can work together with people of other religions to build a better world for all.

1

BREAKING
THE SILENCE

A visitor was wandering around a cemetery one day and came upon a gravestone with these words engraved on it:

COME FOLLOW ME

Beneath this inscription someone had scribbled the following:

"To follow you, I'm not content
Until I know which way you went."

The person who wrote those words was definitely concerned about where he/she would spend eternity and was eager to avoid the fires of Hell. And that person has plenty of company even today. In her book, *The History of Hell,* published in 1993, Alice Turner refers to a Gallup Poll which found that 60 percent of Americans believe in Hell. But what do these people believe *about* Hell?

I have no way of knowing the answer to that question, but I did an informal survey that may give some clues. In the Spring of 2002, I taught an adult church school class at University Presbyterian Church in Austin, Texas, where I presently serve as Parish Associate. The subject for the class was "Taking a Closer Look at Hell." At the first session, I asked the class to tell me what they believed by filling out a survey of beliefs and attitudes about Hell. To get a fuller picture, I gave the same survey to other members of the congregation. I also asked the Presbyterian ministers in our area and the faculty and student body of Austin Presbyterian Theological Seminary to respond to the survey. The results were very interesting and the survey served as a good introduction to the subject.

So I invite you to begin your exploration in the same way. Fill out the survey below, and then come back to it after you have read this book to see if you understand your answers in the same way or if, perhaps, your answers have changed.

A SURVEY OF BELIEFS & ATTITUDES ABOUT HELL

Circle the response that most nearly matches how you would answer the question. If you cannot narrow your choice to one answer, you may circle other answers but try to limit yourself as much as possible.

1. What is Hell?
    A. Separation from God.
    B. A metaphor for God's judgment.
    C. A theological "stick" (i.e., punishment).
    D. An outdated concept.
    E. A lake of fire in which the damned are tormented for eternity.

    F. A present reality from which God offers the power to escape.

2. What is the purpose of Hell?
    A. Eternal Punishment.
    B. Refining and purifying leading to reunion with God.
    C. Punishing and refining leading to reunion with God.
    D. A present awareness that calls us to seek help to overcome the forces that are destroying our life.
    E. Serves no useful purpose.

3. Who is going to Hell?
    A. Those who fail to show love and mercy.
    B. Those who fail to care for the poor.
    C. Those who are unjust and unfair.
    D. Those who do not profess their faith in Jesus Christ.
    E. Only the most evil – Hitler, serial killers, etc.
    F. No one.

4. Upon which biblical images do you base your belief in who is going to Hell?
    A. Jesus' story of the rich man and the beggar, Lazarus, found in Luke 16:19–31. The rich man had everything in this life; the beggar was poor and ill. The rich man finds himself in Hell; the beggar ends up in Heaven.
    B. Jesus' picture of the Last Judgment in Matthew 25:31–46. The King in Jesus' story says, "You that are accursed, depart from me into the eternal fire prepared for the devil and his angels; for I was hungry and you gave me no food, I was thirsty and you gave

me nothing to drink, I was a stranger and you did
not welcome me, naked and you did not give me
clothing, sick and in prison and you did not visit me."

C. Jesus' description of God's love, in John 3:16, that
"God so loved the world that he sacrificed his only
begotten son" in the familiar words of the Authorized
(King James) Version.

D. Paul's advice to the Philippian jailer, in Acts 16:30–31.
"What must I do to be saved?" the jailer asked.
Paul replied, "Believe in the Lord Jesus and you will
be saved, you and your household."

E. Other: (write in your own biblical reference) _____
_____

5. When the biblical writers talk about being saved, what are
we saved from?
A. Hell as a place of future punishment.
B. Ourselves.
C. Things that enslave us – fear, greed, addictive
habits, etc.
D. Loneliness, despair, hopelessness.
E. Meaninglessness.
F. Inability to trust.

6. As you think of your relatives and friends, do you believe
that any of them are going to Hell?
A. Some.
B. None.
C. I would not presume to judge.

7. As you think of your relatives and friends, do you believe
that some of them are controlled by forces that make their

life "hellish"?

A. Some.

B. None.

C. I am not sure about others, but I have experienced Hell as a present reality in my life.

8. Because it is difficult to think about Hell without thinking about its counterpoint, Heaven, when you think of Heaven, what is the primary image that comes to your mind?

A. A place where God reigns.

B. A vision for God's kingdom on earth.

C. A dwelling place for the deceased faithful.

D. A metaphor for God's eternal care and compassion.

E. A theological "carrot" (i.e., a reward).

9. Where did you get your concept of Hell?

A. From the Bible.

B. From your parents.

C. From literature – Dante, Milton.

D. From TV evangelists.

E. Have no concept of Hell.

10 How important do you think discussions of the afterlife are for Christian theology? On a scale of 1–10 (in which "10" signifies very important and "1" signifies not important) rate the theological significance of discussions of the afterlife.

NOT IMPORTANT   VERY IMPORTANT

1..... 2..... 3..... 4..... 5..... 6..... 7..... 8..... 9..... 10

The class and I learned that the 141 people who participated in the survey held many different understandings and beliefs about Hell. Even among clergy and seminary faculty and students, the responses to each question varied greatly. For instance, in response to the first question, the majority of respondents said that Hell is separation from God, but some thought that it is a lake of fire, while others answered that Hell is a present reality from which God offers the power to escape. A few even thought of Hell as an outdated concept or a theological "stick." In Appendix A you will find a tabulation of all of the responses to this broadly unscientific but very useful survey.

The lack of uniformity in the responses to this survey might lead to the conclusion that because there is no uniformly held understanding of Hell, it has lost some of its power to frighten. And on one level, it has. Several years ago, when my wife and I were traveling in England, we visited the ruins of what was once a large and thriving abbey. Rievaulx Abbey is located in a rural area several miles from York. I asked our guide how the monks who ran the abbey were able to amass the funds necessary to build the beautiful church and quarters for those who lived there. The guide said that it was quite simple. The abbot would go to a farmer who lived in that region and request that he donate a portion of his land to the abbey. If the farmer hesitated or refused, the abbot would remind him of the horrors of Hell and imply that the monks might fail to pray for his soul. That threat of being cut off from the prayers of those whom the farmer believed held the keys to Heaven and Hell usually brought forth the requested donation.

Today that kind of threat would be much less effective.

It would not carry as much weight today because the threat of being sent to Hell by a representative of the church would cause very little anxiety for most people. Today, even the Roman Catholic Church has lost enough authority that most of its members would not lose much sleep over such a threat. For instance, despite the church's warning that it is a mortal sin to use any kind of birth control other than the rhythm method, a large majority of North American Roman Catholics practice artificial birth control. Obviously, the fear of being sent to Hell is not so great as the desire to enjoy sexual relations for something other than procreation.

In the 1920s my father was told that he would be barred from the sacraments if his wife-to-be refused to be married by a priest. My mother was unwilling to be married by the priest because she could not in good conscience sign a paper that obligated her to raise their children in the Roman Catholic Church. Although he was a devout Roman Catholic and knew that being cut off from the sacraments sentenced him to Hell, my father chose to marry the woman he loved and suffer the consequences later. I do not believe he went to Hell.

Actually, two things probably tempered Dad's fear of Hell. First, Hell seemed a long time away. When Hell is couched in terms of the life to come, rather than a present reality, it loses much of its power to dissuade. Most people find it difficult to contemplate their own death, much less their eternal destiny. These days, when the church threatens people with something that will become a reality only after their deaths and that has no present consequences, it has a hard sell.

My father's fear of Hell was also tempered by the fact that he was a very rational person. I am sure it was at that moment, when he was being rejected by the church he loved, that he began to question the teachings and authority of the church of his boyhood. My mother was a kind and devout woman and my father must have begun to wonder why his church felt that because she was a Protestant she was going to Hell. Why must he be consigned to Hell simply because he married a woman who would not agree to raise their children in his Roman Catholicism?

It would seem then that, for all practical purposes, Hell has lost its grip on the majority of people. However, appearances may be deceiving. For many people Hell is still a reality that has a great impact upon their thinking and their actions.

This was certainly the case with Andrea Yates, the mother in Houston, Texas, who drowned her five children. The day after Yates was taken to jail, she told a psychiatrist that her bad mothering had made the kids "not righteous," and, as a result, they would "perish in the fires of Hell." She was convinced that if she killed them while they were still young, God would show mercy on their souls.

The jury in this widely publicized case ultimately found Yates guilty of murder, but she was spared the death penalty and sentenced to spend the rest of her life in a mental institution. Most observers believed that Andrea was mentally ill, but little was said about the pastor who planted the concept of Hell that led to the death of these five children. Because of his teachings, Hell was a very vivid reality for this young woman!

However, for the great majority of those who continue to believe firmly in the everlasting fires of Hell, much of the fear has been removed because they believe that they have discovered the way (often the only way) to avoid Hell. They are convinced that all one must do to be saved from Hell is to profess his/her faith in Jesus Christ. I will look at length at this conviction later in the book, but suffice it to say at this point that many conservative, evangelical Christians firmly believe that eternal punishment awaits those who refuse to accept Christ as their Lord and Savior, and the way to avoid that punishment is to accept Jesus' sacrifice to God on our behalf.

Some who hold this position about Hell profess an utter confidence that they will be numbered among the saved and will thus avoid eternal punishment. However, others still have a nagging concern that they may not have believed all the right things. This may sound strange, because the only stated requirement for salvation is to believe that Jesus is the Son of God and the source of our reconciliation with God. However, someone keeps adding more requirements. You must also believe that Jesus was born of a virgin. You must believe that the scriptures are the inerrant word of God. You must believe in the bodily resurrection of Jesus. You must be baptized in a certain way. On and on the list of other requirements goes and some begin to wonder if they have really met all the additional requirements to avoid the wrath of God.

When I was in high school in the late 1940s, I took a trip with two classmates. The three of us were lifeguards for a group of Brownies. As we rode in the back of the bus, we started talking about religion. One of my friends was a Roman Catholic who planned on becoming a nun. The other was a devout member of the Church of Christ. As we talked, my friends found that they could agree on one thing; namely, that because I was not a member of their particular church I was going to Hell. What they could not agree upon was which one was going with me.

When that conversation took place, the official teaching of the Roman Catholic Church was (and still officially is) that there is no salvation outside the Roman Catholic Church (its doctrine of *Extra ecclesiam nulla salus* – Outside the Church, no salvation). Likewise, my Church of Christ friend felt strongly that there was no salvation outside *her* church. So even a profession of faith in Jesus Christ was no guarantee of escaping Hell.

And the uneasiness doesn't end there. Those who read their Bibles carefully begin to note that Jesus spoke frequently about how our failure to care for the poor and to show compassion for the downtrodden could be a cause for ending up in Hell or being sent away into eternal punishment (see the story of the rich man and Lazarus in Luke 16:19–31, and the scene that Jesus paints of the last judgment in Matthew 25:31–46). These stories can certainly lead to considerable doubts about where we will spend eternity. Have we done enough for our brothers and sisters who are in need? Are we among the wealthy who will find it extremely difficult to enter the Kingdom of Heaven?

And Jesus said that there were other things that could bring us down to Hell. In the Sermon on the Mount, he warned that being angry with our brother and calling him a "fool" would make us liable to "the hell of fire." (Matthew 5:22) Just a little later in that same sermon he warned us men that looking at a woman and lusting after her means that we have committed adultery in our hearts. Then, he added, "If your right eye causes you to sin, tear it out and throw it away; it is better for you to lose one of your members than for your whole body to be thrown into Hell." (Matthew 5:29)

In both of these passages, the word Jesus uses for Hell is "Gehenna" – an area just outside Jerusalem where garbage was dumped and where the fires that burned that garbage never went out. This is possibly how the idea of eternal fires entered the concept of Hell.

No wonder, then, that Hell is for many people today a great source of concern. They are fearful and anxious because there appear to be multiple avenues to Hell and they are not sure that they have discovered the foolproof way of avoiding it.

And I am convinced that, on a subliminal level, the threat of a place of eternal torment stills haunts some who like to think that they have outgrown the idea of Hell. Even in more liberal churches the concept of Hell still shapes much of how the Christian faith is presented in our liturgy and our hymns. One Sunday recently at University Presbyterian, we were singing Charles Wesley's hymn, "Rejoice, the Lord is King." As we sang, the words leaped out at me (my emphasis in italics):

God's kingdom cannot fail,
Christ rules o'er earth and heaven;
The keys of death and hell
Are to our Jesus given:

Rejoice in glorious hope!
For Christ, the Judge, shall come
To glorify the saints
For their eternal home:

Here is a hymn which says very plainly that Jesus holds the keys to hell, and that he will come as judge to take the saints to their eternal home – and obviously, though not explicitly stated, to send the wicked to their eternal destiny in Hell.

Most of the people who sang that hymn weren't paying attention to the words, but the hymn writer's theology was making its impact nonetheless. The words were sinking deep into the subconscious mind of the singer and, for some, forming a part of the belief system of that person. Thus, Hell still has great power and influence even if it doesn't get the attention that it once did from the pulpit.

Actually, the fact that Hell doesn't get the attention in our sermons and in our teaching that it once commanded is a major part of the problem. There are some, particularly fundamentalists and conservatives in all the major religions, who profess to know everything there is to know about Hell. They can tell you who is going there, where Hell is located, what the temperature is, and why some are headed for eternal punishment. The problem lies with liberal and moderate Christian pastors and theologians who never say anything about Hell, and who thus leave their congregations and the rest of the world with no way to understand Hell, other than what they hear from TV evangelists and their more conservative friends.

I spoke recently with Scott Black Johnson while he was Professor of Homiletics at Austin Presbyterian Theological Seminary. Dr. Johnson is writing a book on preaching about Heaven and Hell. As we talked, we agreed that most Presbyterians (and probably most United Methodists, Lutherans, and Episcopalians) haven't heard a sermon on Hell in decades.

Unfortunately, Hell won't go away simply by ignoring it. So, I invite you in this book to think about Hell in the hope that we can find a new understanding of Hell that is biblically based and theologically informed. I undertake this task for four major reasons.

First, the concept of Hell is inconsistent with the biblical message of God's long love affair with humanity. Hell, as a place of eternal punishment, does not fit with God's struggle to enable human beings to be what God intends for them to be. It limits God's redemptive effort to one short lifespan. It does not square with the unfolding drama of the Bible in which God works patiently with people and nations to bring about redemptive changes. Hell as punitive rather than redemptive goes against the overall message of scripture. Finally, the punishment doesn't fit the crime – that is, the sentence of *eternal* suffering is too severe for whatever bad things a person may have committed in his/her short lifespan on earth, no matter how terrible the crime.

As I was surfing the Internet one day, I came across a website called BibleHelp.org. One of their entries asked the question, "Is Hell really for Eternity?" The answer according to the person writing this piece is "Yes." The writer then lists the following verses:

Matthew 25:46	"They will go away to *eternal* punishment."
Hebrews 6:2	"The resurrection of the dead, and *eternal* judgment."
Jude 7	The people of Sodom and Gomorrah serve as an example of those who suffer the "punishment of *eternal* fires."
Daniel 12:2	"Some to everlasting life, others to shame and *everlasting* contempt."
2 Thessalonians 1:9	"They will be punished with *everlasting* destruction."
Galatians 1:8	If someone preaches another gospel, he is to be "*eternally* condemned."
Isaiah 66:24	Those who rebelled against God, "Their worm *will not die, nor will the fire be quenched.*"

Revelation 14:10–11   "And the smoke of their torment *rises for ever and ever*."

Mark 3:29   Those who blaspheme will be guilty of an "*eternal* sin."

Isaiah 34:8–10   "Lord has a day of vengeance… It will not be quenched night or day. Its smoke will rise *forever*."

After having listed these texts, the author says, "Although I would love to believe Hell is only a temporary punishment for humans, I cannot find any verses to indicate it. I do not like the idea of a person being punished for eternity, especially the 'sweet old grandmother' who is there simply because she is an unbeliever. As much as I dislike the concept of eternal punishment, I have to abide by what the Bible teaches."

I have two problems with the author of this article.

First, he has found ten proof-texts upon which he bases a belief that is repugnant to him, and he has ignored the message of the Bible as a whole that pictures a God who loves and cares for human beings even when they fail to return that love and do destructive and hurtful things to each other and to themselves.

Second, the writer is repulsed by the notion of Hell as eternal punishment, and yet he believes that God is less repulsed by the notion than he is. In other words, the writer considers himself more compassionate and concerned about human beings than God is. That puzzles me, for if I, as an imperfect parent, cannot conceive of totally rejecting my children and sending them to a place of eternal torment, how can I conceive of a God, whose love far exceeds mine, doing such a thing? Yet the writer of this piece is able to do just that!

Which leads me to my second reason for tackling this subject. **The concept of Hell, as it is often presented in the Christian faith, leads to a far too narrow view of God's grace and saving activity.** It is inconceivable to me that the Creator of the universe, the architect of this small planet, the parent of all humanity, would limit the divine effort to heal a broken world and build a kingdom of peace and love on this earth to one small clan of people who came to be called the Jews. I cannot imagine a God who sends only one messenger to embody the divine love and to teach people the true essence of God, so that they may cease their fear of God and find their peace in God's presence. It seems to me to be the height of arrogance to believe that God has only revealed God's self to my particular religious group and that the rest of the world is damned because they have not yet heard of this particular revelation, or have not suitably responded to it if they have heard.

Religious exclusivity is the root cause of much of the conflict that engulfs our world. And the Christian doctrine of Hell, as it is so often presented, stands at the heart of that exclusivity!

And that leads me to my third reason for exploring this subject. **I am convinced that the concept of Hell as eternal punishment leads to an image of God that has turned many thoughtful people away from the Christian faith.** This was certainly true of a man named Robert G. Ingersoll. Born in 1833, Ingersoll was the son of a Presbyterian minister who, as a single parent, raised him after his mother died during the boy's early childhood. Robert was a brilliant young man who read through the Bible several times and could hold his own in discussions with his father's colleagues. In 1896, he wrote a paper entitled, "Why I Am Agnostic." As I read that paper, I found it voiced eloquently the difficulty and revulsion many thoughtful people have as they confront the concept of Hell and the picture of God that it connotes.

As Ingersoll read about some of the atrocities attributed to God in the Old Testament, he was greatly disturbed by the picture of God that it paints. When he was assured that this happened under the "old dispensation" of unyielding law, but now under the "new dispensation" God is revealed in Christ as merciful and forgiving, he replied, "As a matter of fact, the New Testament is infinitely worse than the Old. In the Old Testament there is no threat of eternal pain. Jehovah had no eternal prison – no everlasting fire. His hatred ended at the grave. His revenge was satisfied when his enemy was dead."[1]

Ingersoll continued (and I have chosen to quote his words directly, although I personally prefer to avoid exclusively masculine references either to God or to human beings):

> In the New Testament, death is not the end, but the beginning of punishment that has no end. In the New Testament, the malice of God is infinite and the hunger of his revenge eternal. The orthodox God, when clothed in human flesh, told his disciples not to resist evil, to love their enemies, and when smitten on one cheek to turn the other, and yet we are told that the same God, with the same loving lips, uttered these heartless, these fiendish words: "Depart ye cursed into everlasting fire, prepared for the devil and his angels." This frightful dogma, this infinite lie, made me the implacable enemy of

Christianity. The truth is that this belief in eternal pain has been the real persecutor. It founded the Inquisition, forged the chains, and furnished the faggots. It has darkened the lives of many millions. It made the cradle as terrible as the coffin. It enslaved nations and shed the blood of countless thousands. It sacrificed the wisest, the bravest and the best.[2]

Ingersoll concluded:

While I have life, as long as I draw breath, I shall deny with all my strength, and hate with every drop of my blood, this infinite lie. Nothing gives me greater joy than to know that this belief in eternal pain is growing weaker every day – that thousands of ministers are ashamed of it. It gives me joy to know that Christians are becoming merciful, so merciful that the fires of hell are burning low – flickering, choked with ashes, destined in a few years to die forever.[3]

This 19th-century thinker would be pleased to know that the concept of Hell as a place of eternal punishment has continued to lose ground among thoughtful theologians and biblical scholars. He would rejoice in the fact that the Roman Catholic Church now speaks of Hell as a separation from God that results from human choice rather than God's sentence. The most recent Catholic catechism says, "To die in mortal sin without repenting and accepting God's merciful love means remaining separate from him for ever *by our own free choice* (emphasis mine). This state of definitive *self-exclusion* (emphasis mine) from communion with God and the blessed is called 'hell.'"[4]

Ingersoll would be gratified that the official teaching of the largest Christian group in the world has repudiated the concept of a vengeful God who throws people into a pit of fire where they will spend eternity. However, he would surely be disturbed by the continued silence of many priests and pastors who fail to address the doctrine of Hell either in their preaching or their teaching. He would find puzzling the fact that the thinking of leading theologians and biblical scholars is rarely shared with laypeople.

Perhaps this reluctance to talk about Hell comes from the fact that any treatment of the subject must include a look at our whole understanding of salvation.

And thus, I come to my fourth reason for wanting to take a closer look at what we believe about Hell. **It is imperative that we re-examine the various theories of the atonement that produce such different understandings of Salvation and of Heaven and Hell.**

What we need to do is look at the bigger picture. What are we saved from? How are we saved? Is salvation a present reality or is it something that we look forward to in the life to come? Are Heaven and Hell to be found only in the next life or do they describe conditions in which we find ourselves right now? All of these questions are tied together and we need to look at them as a whole if we are ever going to understand them individually.

Theology is the discipline that looks at the big picture and I will ultimately turn to this discipline in our search for a new understanding of Hell. But, before I move to the big picture, I invite you to look at some of the pieces of the puzzle. In chapter two, I will present a very brief history of Hell as it evolved in several ancient cultures, including the Israelites, and show how this influenced Jesus' understanding of Hell. From there I will move on in chapter three to look at a theory of the atonement that spawned an image of God and a view of Hell which Jesus never intended. In chapter four, I will look at God's saving activity as it is revealed in the history of the Hebrews and then explore other theories of the atonement and how they inform our understanding of Hell. Chapter five will focus on the ways in which we and society as a whole experience Hell as a present reality. Chapter six will look at Hell's counterpoint, Heaven. Chapter seven will take a brief look at the origin of evil and how we respond to it. Finally, I will draw some conclusions in chapter eight that will, I hope, reflect a deeper and more meaningful understanding of Hell.

2

A BRIEF HISTORY
OF HELL

The idea of Hell did not originate with Judaism or with Christianity. In fact, our Israelite ancestors had only a shadowy concept of life after death and no belief in a place of reward or punishment until sometime around 300 BC. In order, then, to understand the origins of the concept of Hell, we have to turn to other ancient people who lived in the region that surrounded the nation of Israel.

The first accounts of the Land of the Dead that contain the concept of Hell were written nearly 4,000 years ago on baked clay tablets. They were found in the Tigris-Euphrates Valley north of the Persian Gulf in Iraq. This area was home to the Sumerians, Akkadians, Babylonians, and neighboring Assyrians who have been grouped together and called Mesopotamians. These people developed surprisingly sophisticated stories of gods and heroes, which greatly influenced later religious thought, myths, literature, and eschatology. Howard Rollin Patch, in his book *The Other World*, lists a number of elements that appear in nearly all known accounts of the underworld. These include a mountain barrier, a river, a boat and boatman, a bridge, gates and guardians, and an important tree.

Out of this area came a lively Sumerian tale that focuses on Inanna, Queen of Heaven and Earth, and her sister Queen Ereshkigal who rules the dead in the Great Below or the Land of No Return. For obscure reasons, Inanna decides to visit her sister, Ereshkigal. Prudently, she informs her counselor of her intentions, telling him what to do if she does not return. Dressed in her most splendid clothes and jewels, she begins her journey to the Underworld. At the first gate she is halted by a guardian who demands that she remove her crown. At each of the next six gates she must give up another article of clothing. Finally, naked and furious, she confronts Ereshkigal, at whom she "flies." Her sister stops her in mid-flight and hangs her from a stake. Three days and nights pass.

Alarmed by Inanna's absence, the faithful vizier petitions the gods for his mistress's release. Reluctantly, Ereshkigal permits her sister to return to the upper world, on the condition that she provides a substitute or ransom for herself. The ransom Inanna sends is Dumuzi, her husband, who has incurred her wrath because he has enjoyed her absence too much. Eventually, a political compromise is reached by requiring Dumuzi to stay below for only six months of the year, if his sister will stand in for him during the other six months.

What we find in this story is the motif called "The Harrowing of Hell" which turns up in many forms throughout history. In it, a living person descends voluntarily to brave the dangers of the Underworld on a quest that may be deeply serious (Orpheus seeks his wife) or it may be seriously misguided (Theseus and Peirithoos attempt to kidnap Persephone).

Technically, it is called the "descent motif." This marvelous tale of Inanna is the earliest of all the descent stories.

The other ancient area to leave us a written record of its concerns about the world beyond the grave is Egypt. Their "Book of the Dead," provided Egyptians with ritual spells and incantations that would ensure a safe trip through the Underworld. The "Book of the Dead" told of a bodily existence after death. It contained an interesting description of the Day of Judgment.

To reach Heaven, your *ka* or vital life-force (which looks exactly like you) and your *ba* or soul would embark in the boat of Ra. This boat traverses the river of the sky (the Milky Way) during each day to arrive at the West at night with its cargo of the newly dead. Agen and Mahaf are the celestial ferrymen. After disembarking, you must go through seven gates, each with a Gatekeeper, a Watcher, and a Herald, whose name you will invoke by consulting your "Book of the Dead." Next you must greet the many mysterious portals of the house of Osiris before they will open to let you pass.

Anubis will escort you to the Hall of Justice where the Scales of Justice are found. There, you will be given a chance to plead the case for your former and continuing existence. Thoth, God of Wisdom, acts as a prosecutor. Osiris, the Judge, sits on a throne. You may be as eloquent and long-winded as you like, but eventually Anibus will place your heart on the scale to weigh it against a feather from the headdress of Matt, Goddess of Truth. If your heart sinks low under the burden of its sin, Ammit will gobble it up. And that will be the end of you.

Any history of Hell that deals with our ancient ancestors would be incomplete without mentioning a prophet by the name of Zoroaster or Zarathustra. Zoroaster lived in the Middle East after the close of the Old Babylonian period. We know practically nothing about him but we do know that he had enormous influence, directly and indirectly, on the history of Christianity and, specifically, of Hell. His teachings were based on the early Vedic faith, from which Hinduism and Buddhism also developed. However, instead of relying on a pantheon of gods, Zoroaster taught a dualistic religion. The divine force of Good, Ahura Mazda, is pitted against Angra Mainyu, the Lord of Lies, who dwells in the darkness of Hell under the earth. From the depths of Hell, the Lord of Lies sends out devils to torment the world. Law, order, and light must oppose darkness, filth, and death. Their conflict is the history of the world, and the object of the conflict is the soul of human beings.

In the teachings of Zoroaster there is also a Day of Judgment. All good deeds are entered in a great ledger as credits, all wicked actions as debits. If the reckoning is negative, "even if the difference is only three tiny acts of wrong," the soul falls into Hell. If the reckoning is positive, a beautiful maiden escorts the soul across the bridge into the House of Song.

I have taken you on this brief tour of three ancient beliefs about Hell for one very important reason – I want **to contrast these concepts of Hell with those of our spiritual ancestors, the people of Israel,** and to show how in tune Jesus was with his spiritual forebears.

Alice Turner begins her book, *The History of Hell*, with the statement, "Human beings all over the world believe in life after death, in the survival of the conscious personality after the body has ceased to function."[5] Her statement is certainly true of most of the people of the earth. But the glaring exception to the rule is the Israelites prior to the 3rd century BC. Unlike their neighbors, our spiritual ancestors – who are also the spiritual ancestors of Jesus – saw no relationship with the dead. They did not worship them, sacrifice to them, try to visit them, hope to reunite with them in an afterlife, nor anticipate any kind of relationship with their God Yahweh after death. The Psalmist summed up the feeling of the Israelites about death in these words:

> My soul is full of troubles, and my life draws
> near to Sheol. I am counted among those who
> go down to the Pit: I am like those who have
> no help, like those forsaken among the dead,
> like the slain that lie in their grave, like those
> whom You remember no more, for they are cut
> off from your hand. (Psalm 88:3–7)

The Hebrew word, Sheol, which is often mistranslated Hell, actually indicates nothing other than the place where a body is laid to rest, except when it is used metaphorically to indicate depression or despair. The Israelites may have shared with their Mesopotamian neighbors some notion of a dry and dusty underground region which housed a shadowy afterlife, but for the most part our spiritual ancestors were much more interested in this life than in the next. For the Israelites, God's blessings were found here and now, not in some existence yet to come. If a man had land, a good wife, many male children, and a long life on this earth, this was evidence of God's pleasure and all that a man could desire.

Admittedly, there are a few passages in the Hebrew Bible which have been cited as evidence that the Israelites did have a concept of life after death and a division between the righteous and the wicked. However, these passages are scattered and form no consistent teaching that would counter the general belief that life ends at the grave. Some scholars suggest they may have been inserted later, as scribes copied and recopied those scriptures.

One particular passage in Isaiah has been cited as proof for both the existence of an Israelite concept of Hell and the fall of the Devil from Heaven. This is how it reads in the King James Version of the Bible:

> Hell from beneath is moved for thee to meet thee at thy coming: it stirreth up the dead for thee, even all the chief ones of the earth; it hath raised up from their thrones all the kings of the nations. All they shall speak and say unto thee, Art thou also become weak as we? Art thou become like unto us? Thy pomp is brought down to the grave, and the noise of thy viols: the worm is spread under thee, and the worms cover thee. How art thou fallen from heaven, O Lucifer, son of the morning! How art thou cut down to the ground, which didst weaken the nations! For thou has said in thine heart, I will ascend into heaven, I will exalt my throne above the stars of God: I will sit also upon the mount of the congregation, in the sides of the north: I will ascend above the heights of the clouds; I will be like the most High. Yet thou shalt be brought down to hell, to the sides of the pit. (Isaiah 14:9–15)

However, the context of this passage indicates that when Isaiah speaks of Lucifer, he is referring not to the Devil, but rather to the King of Babylon. Isaiah makes it clear to whom these words are addressed when he says (in verse 4 of this chapter) that what follows is a proverb or, as the Revised Standard Version puts it, a "taunt," aimed at the King of Babylon. With this in mind, we realize that the message sent by the prophet of Israel is exactly the same as the one delivered in the Gilgamesh Epic – namely, that proud and ruthless kings will be brought low in Ereshkigal's domain. Actually, the prophet appears to be making a grim joke by sending a Babylonian King to a Babylonian Hell!

Not until the period beginning 300 years before the birth of Jesus did the Jews begin to develop a concept of afterlife that included both punishment and reward. In this time frame, called the "inter-testament period," the Jews were dominated by foreign powers. Faithfulness to Jewish ceremonial laws became a major issue.

During this period, Jews were faced with death if they refused to bow to idols or to eat foods prohibited by their laws. They developed a concept of rewards for the faithful and punishment for those who abandoned the ceremonies of their faith, in order to save their lives.

The Book of II Maccabees describes the revolt of the Jews against their Syrian oppressors. The seventh chapter of that Book contains a gruesome account of the torture and execution of seven pious Jewish brothers and their mother. The dying statements of brothers number three, four, and seven, and also of their mother, all indicate confidence that their mutilated bodies will be resurrected whole by Yahweh – who will also wreak vengeance upon their tormentors.

This theme is also found in the Book of Daniel, which was written around 165 BC. It is clearly stated in Daniel 12: 2–3: "And many who sleep in the dust of the earth shall awake, some to everlasting life and some to shame and everlasting contempt."

To complete the picture of this time period, Josephus, a prominent member of Jerusalem's priestly aristocracy in the 1st century AD, reported that there was a debate about the afterlife among the three major religious groups in the years just before and after Jesus' death. The Sadducees, members of the elite of that day, denied the immortality of the soul and, therefore, any need for reward or punishment. The Pharisees, who were more aligned with the common people, argued that there was a resurrection and that the soul which survives death receives either the reward of a new life in another body or eternal punishment in the underworld. The Essenes, who numbered probably only about four thousand people, agreed with the Pharisees. Josephus attributed their bravery in battle, in part, to their belief in the immortality of the soul. The Essenes shared with the Greeks the idea that after death the souls of the good reside on Isles of the Blessed, whereas the souls of the wicked are tormented forever in a dark, gloomy dungeon.

Alan Bernstein in his book *The Formation of Hell* writes, "No correct understanding of Hell is possible without taking into account the conceptual background of the ancient world prior to Christianity."[6] That is certainly correct. So, with this historical background in mind, I now want to look at how it shaped and influenced Jesus' understanding of Hell. Jesus was a Jew, and like the Jews of his time, he was undoubtedly influenced by the concepts of afterlife and of reward and punishment that came from many sources and cultures in the past and more recent times.

As I read the teachings of Jesus, I am convinced that he was true to the more ancient beliefs of the Israelites that stressed the importance of God's blessings in this present life. In other words, his was not an *otherworldly* message or mission. In fact, Jesus himself stated the purpose of his mission at the beginning of his ministry during his remarks in the synagogue in Nazareth. Taking the book of the prophet Isaiah, he read this passage:

> The Spirit of the Lord is upon me,
> Because God has anointed me
> To bring good news to the poor.
> He has sent me to proclaim
> Release to the captives
> And recovery of sight to the blind,
> To let the oppressed go free,
> To proclaim the year of the Lord's favor.
> (Luke 4:18,19)

Having read these words, Jesus said, "Today this scripture has been fulfilled in your hearing." (Luke 4:21)

Jesus understood his mission as revealing the compassion and concern of God for the less fortunate of the earth and calling those who had wealth and power and resources to act as God's agents in relieving suffering and securing economic and political justice. In pursuit of that mission, he went about healing the sick, feeding the hungry, showing personal concern for the leper and the outcast, and associating with those who had been rejected by the mainstream of society. His mission was to create a just and loving society on this earth, to make life meaningful and to fill it full of joy. He said, "I have come that they might have life and have it abundantly." (John 10:10)

In other words, he came to announce that the Kingdom of God had arrived with his coming, and to call all of us to work to make that Kingdom a reality on earth even as we pray, "Thy Kingdom come, Thy will be done on earth, even as it is in Heaven."

If we accept this as Jesus' understanding of his mission, then we can begin to see how he used the concepts of Heaven and Hell to promote this vision, and to ensure we understood how important it is to our Creator. Hans Küng, a Roman Catholic theologian, makes this point when he says,

> The New Testament statements about Hell are not meant to supply information about a hereafter to satisfy curiosity or fantasy. They are meant to bring vividly before us here and now the absolute seriousness of God's claim and the urgency of conversion in the present life.[7]

In that sense, Jesus used the promise of Heaven and the threat of Hell just as the prophets of Israel and the Jewish leaders in the 1st and 2nd century BC had used them.

Except with Jesus, there were two major differences. Unlike the Maccabees and the Book of Daniel, Jesus' concern was not ceremonial purity and right beliefs. His concern was social justice and right relations among human beings. Thus, in his parable of the Last Judgment, the issue is not ritual or moral purity or impurity. The thing that gets you sent to Hell is your failure to feed the hungry, to clothe the naked, to visit the sick, etc. What gets you to Heaven is your faithfulness in showing the compassion of God to those who are sick, hungry, in need of clothing…

This concern for social justice and for compassion is repeated again and again in Jesus' teachings. I am convinced that he did not use the threat of Hell primarily to warn people of the eternal consequences of their failure to seek justice and to show compassion. He used the threat of Hell as a way to warn people that their survival and happiness on this earth is predicated by God on the willingness of the rich and powerful to care for and treat justly those who are less affluent and powerful.

This reflects the primary message of the prophets of Israel (writing mostly six to eight centuries before Jesus' time) who constantly warned that God required justice and mercy. In the absence of those virtues, they prophesied, the Israelites would end up as a slave people living in exile and misery in a foreign country.

Jesus was concerned about making this life as harmonious and productive as possible. God is our Creator and our Parent. As such, God expects us to live together and work together for the betterment of the human family here and now.

But Jesus also saw beyond this life, and the image he used to portray life in that future existence was the family. By his resurrection Jesus reveals the eternal dimension of our relationship with our Creator. He assures us there is a life after this earthly existence, but he has redefined what that life will be like. It is not divided into the blessed and the damned, into Heaven and Hell. Rather, the imagery is that of a banquet hall in the household of God to which we are all invited. Some of the family may absent themselves for a while. If we choose to leave home, as did the prodigal son in Jesus' famous parable in Luke's gospel, our heavenly parent grieves. But note in that parable that the father did not drive the prodigal out of the house. Rather, the prodigal chose to leave. God – like the loving father in this story, or the shepherd with the lost sheep, or the widow with the lost coin – rejoices when that which was lost is found, when the one who has left home returns. And note that in this story the father throws a banquet when his son comes home.

However, homecoming isn't for everyone right away – not because some have not been invited or have been barred from the family table, but because they feel no love for the Creator or for the other members of the family. That is their choice, not God's, because God's love is always waiting for them and the heavenly parent longs for all to come home. Indeed, the whole thrust of scripture is that God will never be satisfied until all of humanity is sitting at the banquet table, and that God will never give up until that is accomplished. In the end, I am convinced that there will be no Hell – no one sitting outside the banquet hall – because God's love will ultimately prevail!

3

THE HELL
JESUS NEVER INTENDED

Now, if what I have just said about Jesus' understanding of Hell is an accurate interpretation of what he taught and what his life and death were all about, how has Hell become such a frightening and destructive concept for so many Christians? How did we end up with a concept of Hell that Jesus never intended and which scripture as a whole will not support?

I, personally, would lay much of the blame at the feet of a man named Anselm who lived in the 11th century. Of course, he did not single-handedly distort Jesus' intention. But he did set forth a way of thinking about the human problem and God's action to remedy that problem which has had enormous influence across the centuries.

Two women who rang my doorbell recently had probably never heard of Anselm, but the message they brought me came straight from his writing so long ago. These women asked me if I had a church home. I told them that I was a Presbyterian minister and that I was presently serving as a Parish Associate at the University Presbyterian Church. That didn't seem to satisfy them as to my salvation, so they asked if they could leave a pamphlet with me. Before I could accept or decline, they handed me the tract and left. The cover of the pamphlet proclaimed in bold letters: "GOD LOVES YOU." Inside was this message (boldface as in the original):

Please do not resent us for giving you this tract. We love your soul, and we want to tell you, if you have never been born again, you are on your journey to a place where you will burn for ever and ever. You see, God commanded Adam not to eat of the tree of knowledge, for in that day he would die. **"And the Lord God commanded the man, saying, Of every tree thou mayest eat; But of the tree of the knowledge of good and evil, thou shalt not eat of it: for in the day that thou eatest thereof thou shalt surely die." Genesis 2: 16–17.** Adam ate of the tree of knowledge and on that day he died spiritually. **"Wherefore, as by one man sin entered into the world, and death by sin; and so death passed upon all men, for that all have sinned." Romans 5: 12.** You are in this same lost condition if you have never been born again. To continue in this lost condition until death takes you from this world, condemns you to a lake of fire. **"And whosoever was not found written in the book of life was cast into the lake of fire." Revelation 20:15.** Jesus loves you. He loved you even before you were born into this world. **"But God commendeth his love toward us, in that, while we were yet sinners, Christ died for us." Romans 5:8.** The love of God for you is greater than all understanding. He prepared a way of salvation to keep you from this lake of fire. **"For God so loved the world, that he gave his only begotten Son, that whosoever believeth in him should not perish, but have everlasting life." John 3:16.** Jesus died upon a cross and shed His blood, so that you could be saved. **"But this man, after he had offered one sacrifice for sins for ever, sat down on the right hand of God." Hebrews 10:12.** Jesus paid it all. Salvation is waiting for everyone who will receive Jesus as their Savior. **"But as many as received him, to them gave he power to become the sons of God, even to them that believe on his name." John 1:12.** Right now, will you bow your head and call on Jesus to save your soul? The decision is yours. **"Then Agrippa said unto Paul, Almost thou persuadest me to be a Christian." Acts 26: 28.** Almost is not good enough. Almost will send you to hell. Call upon Jesus today to save your soul.

The message of that pamphlet comes directly from Anselm. Protestant Reformers only slightly modified his teaching. In a book called *Cur Deus Homo* (Why God Became Man) written in 1098 while he was archbishop of Canterbury, Anselm set out a theory of the atonement that makes God a feudal lord and that sets up the necessity of eternal punishment for those who offend the honor of this all-powerful one.

Anselm's argument went like this. Adam sinned against God in eating the forbidden fruit in the Garden of Eden. By this act of disobedience, Adam offended the honor of the Sovereign Lord by disturbing the order and beauty of the universe. Adam's sin was passed on to all succeeding generations through the act of procreation (this is what has been called "Original Sin"). Thus all human beings are born in sin, stand guilty in the sight of God, and are automatically condemned to Hell. Since they are all guilty, human beings have nothing they can offer God to restore the divine harmony of creation and escape the fires of Hell. If human beings are to be forgiven by God, God must provide the means by which restitution can be made. So, God sends his Son, Jesus. Jesus, being born of a virgin, is thus not tainted with the original sin of Adam. Furthermore, Jesus lives a perfect life and therefore is not subject to death, the penalty God imposed on Adam for sinning. When Jesus gives his life, in a death on the Cross that he does not deserve, he builds up a balance of merits which can be credited to all those who believe in him. Since Jesus is a human being, this fulfills the requirement that a man offer an acceptable sacrifice on behalf of other human beings. And because Jesus is also God, the gift of his life to God fulfills the requirement that someone of equal status with the Sovereign Lord make amends.

In this convoluted argument, Anselm answers the question that he raises in the title of his book. Why was it necessary for God to become human? Because Jesus must be *both* divine and human. A human being must make restitution for humanity's failure to honor God's created order of justice and harmony.

Yet only someone who is also divine can offer a sacrifice that would be acceptable to the Lord of the Universe.

Belief in Jesus, then, becomes the only way to escape Hell and to find the key to Heaven because only Jesus fulfills the requirement of being "both God and Man."

In the 11th century when Anselm wrote, these images made good sense to a people who lived in a feudal society. The predominant image of authority was the king or ruler who had the power of life and death over those who lived in his territory. Author James Carroll reminds us,

> We are in a rigidly juridical world here, with God as an aggrieved feudal lord, carefully weighing out recompense on a finely calibrated scale. This was very much the world of Anselm, who was forced to play out in his own life, both in Urban II's behalf and in his own as archbishop of Canterbury, a version of the feudal dispute that set Pope Gregory VII against Emperor Henry IV.[8]

Anselm, like most of us, could not transcend his culture and his immediate circumstances. Therefore, he gave us a picture of a God whose chief concern is justice and honor, because those were the concerns of both the secular and ecclesiastical powers of his day. And because power has always appealed to people, this picture of a God who demands perfect obedience and who imposes awful consequences for disobedience prevails to this day.

One of the chief creeds of the denomination that I have served as a pastor for over forty years still echoes Anselm's teaching. In the *Westminster Confession of Faith*, we read:

> The Lord Jesus, by His perfect obedience
> and sacrifice of Himself, which He through
> the eternal Spirit once offered up unto God,
> *hath fully satisfied the justice of His father*,
> and purchased not only reconciliation, but
> an everlasting inheritance in the kingdom of
> heaven, for all those whom the Father hath
> given Him. (VIII, 5, emphasis mine)

This portrait of God is frightening for many because love that must be bought at the price of a violent death on the Cross hardly sounds like love. Carroll reacts to this portrayal of God by saying, "Whatever the feudal origins of the system, however tenderly meant its composition, and however glibly we invoke the word 'love,' the God of such atonement can appear, in a certain light, to be a monster."[9]

This opinion is echoed by Rita Nakashima Brock when she writes, "The shadow of omnipotence haunts atonement. The ghost of the punitive father lurks in the corners. He never disappears even as he is transformed into the image of forgiving grace."[10]

Walter Wink is even harsher in his judgment of the picture of God found in this doctrine of the atonement. He says, "The nonviolent God of Jesus becomes a God of unequaled violence, since God not only allegedly demands the blood of the victim who is most precious to him, but holds humanity accountable for a death that God both anticipates and requires. Against such an image of God the revolt of atheism is an act of pure religion!"[11]

Wink's remarks sum up my own reaction to Mel Gibson's movie, *The Passion of the Christ,* released at the beginning of Lent in 2004. In an interview with Diane Sawyer, Gibson quoted a portion of a sentence from the 53rd chapter of Isaiah which says, "And with his stripes we are healed." Gibson used the prophet's words to justify a ten-minute scene in the movie which shows Jesus being beaten mercilessly by the Roman soldiers before his crucifixion. It is a horrifying scene. Evidently, for the producer, it showed Jesus receiving the scourging from God that we deserve.

When I heard that explanation, I decided that this movie perpetuated an understanding of the atonement that has driven many people away from the Christian faith. The movie tried to show the depth of God's love, but ended up making God a ruthless disciplinarian who would not be satisfied until God had received the required pound of flesh. I had no desire to see this movie.

Shirley Guthrie, Jr. was professor of systematic theology at Columbia Theological Seminary in Decatur, Georgia, until his recent retirement. In his book *Christian Doctrine,* he tells a story which illustrates how Anselm's theory is often presented and how frightening it can be. This is his story:

> Once upon a time a boy went to a revival
> meeting. He had grown up in a Christian home
> and in the church, but he heard something that
> night he had never heard before. The preacher
> held up a very dirty water glass.
>
> "See this glass? That's you. Filthy, stained
> with sin, inside and out."
>
> He picked up a hammer.

"This hammer is the righteousness of God. It is the instrument of his wrath against sinful men. *His justice can be satisfied* (emphasis mine) only by punishing and destroying sinners whose lives are filled with vileness and corruption."

He put the glass on the pulpit and slowly, deliberately drew back the hammer clinched in his fist, took deadly aim, and with all his might let the blow fall.

But a miracle happened! At the last moment the preacher covered the glass with a pan. The hammer struck with a crash that echoed through the hushed church. He held up the untouched glass with one hand and the mangled pan with the other and made his point.

"Jesus Christ died for your sins. He took the punishment which ought to have fallen on you. *He satisfied the righteousness of God* (emphasis mine) so that you might go free if you believe in him."

When the boy went to bed that night, he could not sleep. Meditating on what he had seen and heard, he decided that he was terribly *afraid* of God. But could he *love* such a God? He could love Jesus, who had sacrificed himself for him. But how could he love a God who wanted to "get" everyone and was only kept from doing it because Jesus got in the way? The thought crossed the boy's mind that he could only hate such a hammer-swinging God who had to be bought off at such a terrible price. But he quickly dismissed the thought, That very God might read his mind and punish him.

Some other thoughts also troubled the boy. Despite what the preacher said about the righteousness of God, is it really right to punish one person for what other people do? And granted that he was a pretty bad boy sometimes, was he really all that bad? Did he really deserve to die? Was he really so sinful that God had to kill Jesus to make up for what he had done?

Finally, he wondered what good it had all done in the end. The glass had escaped being smashed to bits, but nothing had really changed. After the drama was over, it was still just as dirty as it was before. Even if Jesus did save him from God, how did Jesus' sacrifice help him to be a different person?[12]

In his story, Guthrie identifies not only the fear that Anselm's portrayal of God engenders but also some of the fallacies that are inherent in his argument. Anselm has been called the father of scholasticism. He defined theology as "faith in search of reason," and I commend him for his effort to explain God's activity so that human minds can comprehend it. But, having said this, I must point out several flaws in his attempt to give a reasoned explanation of what God was doing in Jesus Christ to save the world from God's wrath.

To begin, Anselm bases his argument on a literal interpretation of the story of Adam and Eve as found in the third chapter of Genesis. In order to justify God's judgment upon all of humanity, he assumes an original couple whose defiance of God's orders was so heinous in the Creator's sight that all succeeding generations could be contaminated with their sin. This interpretation has three problems.

First, Adam and Eve were not a literal couple who lived approximately 6,000 years ago and from whom all humanity originated. The biblical storyteller makes that evident by using the name "Adam" for the man in this story. "Adam" in the Hebrew means human being or humankind. It is not the name of one person. Rather, it indicates that the person in this story represents all human beings. Through the myth of Adam and Eve, the ancient storyteller tried to define the divine origins of the human race and the difficulties, burdens, strife, alienation, and discord that exist between human beings and their Creator.

Since there was never an original couple named Adam and Eve, there can be no original sin. Matthew Fox reminds us that the concept of original sin is not found in Jewish thought. He writes, "Even though the Jewish people knew Genesis for a thousand years before Christians, they do not read original sin into it. As the twentieth-century Jewish prophet, Elie Wiesel points out, 'the concept of original sin is alien to Jewish tradition.'"[13]

Fox reminds us that infants enter a torn and broken world, but he adds, "We do not enter as blotches on existence, as sinful creatures, we burst into the world as 'original blessings'." Fox quotes Herbert Haag, former president of the Catholic Bible Association of Germany and author of *Is Original Sin in Scripture?* According to Haag,

No man [sic] enters the world a sinner. As a creature and image of God he is from his first hour surrounded by God's fatherly love. Consequently, he is not at birth, as is often maintained, an enemy of God and a child of God's wrath. A man becomes a sinner only through his own individual and responsible action.[14]

Rabbi Harold Kushner goes so far as to see in the story of Adam and Eve a positive rather than a negative message. "I would like to suggest another way of reading the story," Kushner writes,

...one that I think makes better sense of the events, leaves fewer loose ends, and paints a more positive picture of our first ancestors and by implication of us as well. We don't have to feel condemned by the story, inevitably fated to sin and lose God's love as Adam and Eve did. We can read it as the inspiring, even liberating story of what a wonderful, complicated, painful, and rewarding thing it is to be a human being. I would like to suggest that the story of the Garden of Eden is a tale, not of Paradise Lost but of Paradise Outgrown, not of Original Sin but of the Birth of Conscience.[15]

My second problem with Anselm's interpretation is that guilt cannot be transmitted from one generation to the next simply through procreation. There are passages of scripture which seem to imply that guilt can be inherited but, once again I argue that this is a misreading of the text. For example, God is reported to have said to Moses, "The Lord, the Lord, a God merciful and gracious, slow to anger, and abounding in steadfast love and faithfulness, keeping steadfast love for the thousandth generation, forgiving iniquity and transgression and sin, yet by no means clearing the guilty, but visiting the iniquity of the parents upon the children and the children's children to the third and fourth generation." (Exodus 34:6–7)

This passage might seem to imply that guilt can be transmitted from one generation to another. But a closer reading makes clear that it is the *consequences of a parent's behavior* that we inherit rather than their guilt. If those who came before acted wisely and in harmony with God's desire for justice and compassion and have been good stewards of the earth, their children will reap the benefits of their behavior. However, if those who have come before us acted unwisely and defied God's commands to love others and to care for the world, we will – and do – suffer the consequences of their actions.

We know all too well the truth of this assertion. We suffer still today the consequences of our forebears' ownership of slaves and their misguided belief that black people were less than fully human. The seeds of present-day racial tensions were sown many years ago. Similarly, if we continue to pollute and destroy our environment today, our children will suffer the consequences of our failure to be good stewards of this earth.

The illustrations could go on and on. We pay for the sins of those who have come before us because we suffer the consequences of their selfishness and misguided choices. But God does not judge us guilty for what those who have preceded us have done.

It is unfair – and in our social system, illegal – to blame the sons and daughters for the transgressions of their parents. That is one of the roots of racial prejudice. And to imply that God declares all of humanity guilty because of the disobedience of an original pair of human beings is to paint an awful picture of God. It may have been true in Anselm's day that a peasant's family could be executed by the feudal lord for something the peasant did, but to say that God works in this manner is to make God an arbitrary and capricious tyrant.

Finally, the third chapter of Genesis was not written to depict the fall of humanity from a state of perfection prior to the disobedience of Adam and Eve. Walter Brueggeman, an Old Testament Professor, writes in his commentary on Genesis, "This text is commonly treated as the account of 'the fall.' Nothing could be more remote from the narrative itself... In general, the Old Testament does not assume such a 'fall.' Deuteronomy 30:11–14 is more characteristic in its assumption that humankind can indeed obey the purposes of God."[16]

There never was a perfect world to fall from. Scientists tell us that the universe is about twenty billion years old. Human beings began to emerge about four million years ago on this planet. There never was a time in the universe or in human history when the world was at peace. Always there was strife and envy, jealousy and hatred, mistrust and greed, fear and loneliness. So God is not concerned about the acts of a primordial couple that spoiled a perfect world. Rather, God is active in human history, and in the great prophets and religious visionaries of the world, enabling human beings to cope with an imperfect world and to grow toward the loving, caring creatures that God longs for us to become.

So much for Anselm's distorted interpretation of the Old Testament. But as Christians, we also have the New Testament. We believe that the love of God was manifest in Jesus Christ in a way that diminishes our fear and mistrust of God and ourselves and each other, so that we become more nearly the kind of people who can live in peace and harmony and care for this marvelous world.

In contrast to Anselm's understanding of God as a feudal lord, Jesus gives us a picture of God as Parent, Father, Mother, Lover, Friend, and Comforter. When we examine the parables and instructions of Jesus, we find that he portrays God most often as "Father." When his disciples asked him to teach them to pray, Jesus gave them a model for their praying which begins, "Our Father…"

Hans Küng points out how revolutionary was Jesus' choice of "Father" for addressing God in this prayer. There are isolated instances in which God is referred to as Father in the Old Testament. But Jesus' use of the Aramaic form *abba* for "Father" in speaking to God is extraordinary. Küng comments,

> *Abba* – like our "Daddy" – is originally a child's word, used however in Jesus' time also as a form of address to their father by grown-up sons and daughters and as an expression of politeness generally to older persons deserving of respect. But to use this not particularly manly expression of tenderness, drawn from the child's vocabulary, this commonplace term of politeness, to use this as a form of addressing God, must have struck Jesus' contemporaries as

irreverent and offensively familiar, very much
as if we were to address God today as "Dad."[17]

Jesus was changing his disciples' concept of God. Completely
absent from the salutation of this prayer are the terms of
obeisance that one would expect in addressing the King of
Heaven, the Lord of the Universe. Jesus gives us a different
image of God. As Küng puts it (still using, at the time his book
was written, exclusively masculine pronouns for God):

> He is not the all-too-masculine God of
> arbitrary power or law. He is not the God
> created in the image of kings and tyrants, of
> hierarchs and schoolmasters. But he is the good
> God — it is difficult to find less trite formulas
> — who identifies himself with men, with their
> needs and hopes. He does not demand but
> gives, does not oppress but raises up, does not
> wound but heals.[18]

Norman Pittenger makes the same paradigm shift in our image
of God. He reminds us that when we speak of God's glory,

> that glory is no majestic enthronement as
> almighty ruler and self-exalted monarch, but is
> the sheer Love-in-act which generously gives,
> graciously receives, and gladly employs whatever
> of worth or value has been accomplished in a
> world where God is faithfully active to create
> more occasions for more good at more times
> and in more places.[19]

One of Jesus' best known parables completes the transformation of God's image. In the parable of the prodigal son, God is pictured as the father who gives his younger son his inheritance when the son asks for it, who watches sadly as the son leaves but does not chase after him, who sees the son returning and runs out to meet him and who finally, interrupting his son's admission of guilt, accepts him back without question, without putting him on probation, and orders his servants to prepare a feast.

The God whom Jesus reveals is a God of infinite, inexhaustible love – not the righteous judge or outraged potentate that atonement theories have painted for us. In this insight, Native Americans could have taught the missionaries who came to convert them. In the book, *A Native American Theology*, the authors tell us, "There is no sense in any Native traditions that reflect any attempt to make God, a god, or the spirits, happy with us or to placate the judgment of God over against a sinful humanity. There is no sense of God's anger."[20]

The authors go on to say, "There were ceremonies to make right an imbalance that we ourselves as pitiful two-leggeds may have instigated – through our laziness, inattention, oversight, anger, or some unknown mistake. But even in such cases, the anger of the spirits is never at stake in most Native traditions when those traditions are understood at their most complex level."[21]

When we discover the God whom Jesus came to reveal, we realize that the objective of Jesus' birth, life, teachings, actions, death, and resurrection is to draw us back to God rather than to pay off a wrathful ruler or an all-righteous judge. When we grasp this new understanding of the atonement, we realize that throughout all of history, God has been seeking to reconcile an alienated humanity so that we can become more nearly what we were created to be. Who Jesus is and what Jesus does is aimed at changing something in us rather than changing something in God.

4

LOOKING AT HELL
THROUGH
A BROADER LENS

Anselm always takes center stage when we examine the concept of Hell because his theory of the atonement has been so widely accepted in the church. One almost forgets that he didn't write his famous book *Cur Deus Homo* until 1098 AD – which means that for thousands of years before Anselm, both Hebrew and Christian thinkers had already been wrestling with how to understand the human predicament and what God has done to address it.

As we look at Hell through a broader lens than the one Anselm offers, we make a startling discovery. For the most part, these inspired thinkers and writers were not concerned with how to placate an angry or vengeful God. Instead, they concentrated on informing their listeners as to how God was working with the people to bring about changes in them and their world that would enable them to escape the Hells they had created for themselves.

The Hebrew Scriptures contain the story of God's relentless search for ways to teach human beings to trust their Creator and to relate to each other with justice and compassion.

The story begins with the choice of a people through whom God intends to bless the whole world. In the biblical narrative, God calls Abraham and Sarah to leave their native country and go to a new land. They are not chosen for their purity or holiness. They are chosen because they are willing to trust this awesome voice that asks them to leave their security and to go on a great adventure for the good of humanity. With the call comes a promise – which we have traditionally called a "Covenant" – from God that out of Sarah and Abraham will come a great nation, which will prove to be a blessing to all the people of the earth.

Years later when these Hebrews found themselves in bondage in Egypt, they cried out to God to deliver them. God secured their release from captivity and led them back to the land that they had originally settled. The Israelites looked upon their deliverance from bondage in Egypt as the supreme example of God's care for them. It became the cornerstone of their faith. Therefore, when God wanted to call these people back to faithfulness and trust, God reminded them that they had once been slaves in Egypt and had been delivered from captivity by Divine intervention. Over and over again, the leaders of Israel said to the people, "Remember that you were a slave in Egypt, and the Lord your God brought you out from there with a mighty hand and an outstretched arm; therefore..." (Deuteronomy 5:15) The "therefore" was always followed by a call to obedience based on what God had already done for them.

When the scattered clans of the Hebrews left Egypt, they were a disorganized band of people who knew little about governing themselves or living together harmoniously. Therefore, God gave to them laws that would remind them of their obligations to their Creator and their obligations to each other. The Ten Commandments and the other laws God helped the Israelites develop were not intended to test the obedience of this chosen people. Rather, they were the gracious gift of God so that these people could find personal fulfillment and joy and become a productive and caring society. When people broke the law, God grieved as a Holy Parent at the misery and suffering they were causing themselves and others.

Thus God did something else. God gave the people prophets who could speak for God, warning the people of the consequences of their disobedience. The prophets acted as the social conscience of the people and pointed out where they had broken the laws God had helped them develop. But the prophets did more than act as a social conscience. They also reminded the people of the mighty acts of God in delivering them, and that their first obligation was to their Creator and Sustainer. The prophet Micah summed up for the people what God required of them when he said,

> He has told you, O mortal, what is good;
> and what does the Lord require of you but to
> do justice, and to love kindness, and to walk
> humbly with your God?" (Micah 6:8)

Significantly, the prophets did not limit their warnings to the common people. They also confronted kings and those who were wealthy, pointing out that when they failed to honor God by not taking care of those in need, they broke the social contract that bound the nation together. Thus Amos addressed the wealthy women of his day as "cows of Bashan" and warned them that God would not tolerate the ways in which they oppressed the poor and crushed those in need. (Amos 4:1–3) For those who failed to show kindness and mercy and to walk humbly with God, the consequence would be the Hell of captivity in a foreign land.

Nathan's confrontation with King David, after David had seduced Bathsheba and had her husband Uriah killed in battle, is a classic example of the fearlessness of the prophets. Even the great King David, whom God loved, must hear of God's displeasure and must suffer the consequences of his despicable acts as he loses the son born to Bathsheba by his crime.

The prophet's job was to dissuade the people from acting in ways that would harm themselves and others and disrupt the social order. But there would be times when the people would break the laws despite all these warnings. So God provided a way to receive forgiveness and reconciliation with God and each other. God gave the people priests. By their role of offering sacrifices, they could reassure offenders that God no longer held their offense against them.

It is important to note something at this point that has great significance for our understanding of Christ's sacrifice on the Cross. It is often claimed that Christ's sacrificial death on the Cross was a payment to God that satisfies God's justice or honor. And the sacrificial system in the Hebrew Bible is cited as a model for what Christ was doing on the Cross. However, a closer look at the sacrifices offered by the Israelites and by their priests shows that the offering did not represent a payment to God. It was, rather, a symbolic recognition that God had already forgiven the penitent person. Nathaniel Micklem makes this point very powerfully in the *Interpreter's Bible*:

How could the blood of bulls and goats be supposed to take away sin? The idea strikes us as barbaric, but there is evidence that at least the spiritually minded Hebrew saw as clearly as we do that the ritual act of sacrifice was not efficacious in itself. We must look deeper. A sacrifice was a gift offered by the worshiper to God. But when one offers a gift and another receives it, a relationship of friendship is created between them. If two are estranged and the one who has done wrong offers a gift, the offended friend, by receiving the gift, signifies that he also receives the giver, and that the enmity is put away... If Israel or the Israelite through some pollution, consciously or unconsciously incurred, felt himself to be estranged from God, what could he do? He could bring a gift. But would it be received? Yes, said the priests as the interpreters and transmitters of the traditions of Israel; the Lord was merciful; he himself had promised that if this or that gift was given in this way or that, he would receive it, and receiving it would be reconciled with the offender. Not magic, but a theology of grace is presupposed.[22]

In the Hebrew Bible, the sacrifice did not represent a payment made to appease or placate an angry God. It was a gift offered to God as a way of saying, "I have done wrong and I am sorry." And the marvelous thing was that those offering the sacrifice had the assurance that if they were sincerely sorry for what they had done, they could be sure that God would accept their gift and that their fractured relationship would be restored.

Additionally, those who had acted immorally or who had taken advantage of the poor knew that God would work with them, if they were sincerely repentant, to heal the social fabric and to save the nation.

Through the sacrificial system, then, God was not looking for a ransom payment or a bribe. Rather, God was looking for evidence of a change of heart on the part of individuals or the nation that would give God the opportunity to work with them to make whole that which was broken and to heal relationships that had become unhealthy. I am convinced that God was also doing just that in Christ's sacrifice on the Cross. I will look at this understanding of the Cross later in this chapter.

God worked tirelessly to build trust in the people of Israel and thus to create a nation that would demonstrate the qualities of compassion and justice to the whole world. Unfortunately, the Israelites often forgot, or chose to ignore, what God had done for them and what God had taught them. Like all societies, their civil and religious leaders became corrupt. Wealth concentrated in the hands of a few, while the great majority lived in poverty. The people forgot God's call to seek justice, to love kindness, and to walk humbly with their God. In time, even the glorious kingdom of David was racked by civil war that tore the country into two weakened fragments. First, the Northern Kingdom of Israel was carried away into captivity and its people ceased to exist as a separate and distinct group. Then, the Southern Kingdom of Judah suffered a similar fate less than two hundred years later.

For the Israelites, being exiles in a foreign country with little hope of ever seeing their homeland again was a form of Hell. There by the rivers of Babylon, as the Psalmist described it, they sat down and wept. There they remembered their homeland, and there they endured the derision of their tormentors. (Psalm 137) Like millions of refugees and displaced persons today who have been driven from their homes, their country, and all that is familiar, these Israelites endured the Hell of despair and hopelessness.

But, in this case, God eventually intervened. A remnant of the people was allowed to return to the land from which they had been deported. The religious leaders of the Jews saw this return from exile as another example of how God never abandons the people, even when they turn their backs on their gracious and loving Creator.

Once again, God is portrayed, not as a cruel judge who condemns those who create their own Hells, but rather as the Holy One who works patiently to rescue those who have reaped the harvest of their own failure. By this intervention, God encourages them to act justly and to trust their Creator's guidance.

The recurring message of the Hebrew Bible is that God is constantly faithful to a people who are often unfaithful. God's steadfast love never wavers, even though those who were chosen to show the world how to live together in a just and compassionate society rarely lived up to their part of the Covenant.

As time passed, those who recognized that they had been chosen as an instrument of God's blessing became so obsessed with their responsibility that they became a living paradox. They became intent upon separating themselves from the rest of the world, thinking that this was the way to please God and to maintain the purity that God demanded of them.

So God sent one more prophet to remind the people that what God desires is not perfect obedience to myriad laws but a people who demonstrate in their individual and corporate life a love for God, a love for themselves, and a love for the rest of humanity. When a young man asked this prophet, Jesus, what he must do to inherit eternal life, he pointed to the ancient law which said, "You shall love the Lord, your God, with all your heart and mind and soul and strength, and you shall love your neighbor as yourself." (Luke 10:27)

The way to eternal life is found in the path of love. Conversely, the way to avoid living death – the Hells that we create for ourselves – is to discover the power of love to transform both the individual and society.

Jesus was a Jew. He loved his people and their heritage and tradition. But he also saw how some of the religious leaders of his day had distorted God's message, turning it into a set of laws that were impossible for people to follow. At one point, Jesus turned to those religious leaders and said to them, "Woe to you, scribes and Pharisees, hypocrites! For you tithe mint, dill, and cumin, and have neglected the weightier matters of the law: justice and mercy and faith." (Matthew 23:23) The religious leaders of Jesus' day had distorted the Jewish faith. They had made it a narrow, exclusive club marked by rigid adherence to the law. They had forgotten their own prophets who had said that God wants justice and kindness rather than mindless obedience and empty sacrifices.

The scribes and Pharisees were not bad people. They believed sincerely that the way to please God lay in perfect obedience to a multitude of laws, which they had refined to insure the purity of God's people. Somehow they had missed the point that the prophets had delivered across the centuries. The laws were not an isolation chamber, a quarantine ward, intended to protect the nation of Israel from contamination by the social cultures around them. The laws were God's gracious provision so that the people might enjoy life and live in peace and harmony. As Jesus pointed out to them, the law of the Sabbath was given for the benefit of human beings rather than human beings being made in order to observe the Sabbath. (Mark 2:23–28)

We have to be careful not to be too hard on the religious leaders of Jesus' day. The early leaders of Christianity and those who followed them have often fallen into the same trap. It is always the tendency of religious leaders to set up rules and teachings that become the acid test of a person's faithfulness to God and thus the path to salvation.

In her book *Witness to the Truth* Edith Hamilton points out how the early church leaders made the same mistake as their Jewish counterparts (my emphasis in italics):

> The fathers of the church were good men, often saintly men, who cared enough for Christ to die for him. *But they did not trust him.* They could not trust the safety of his church to his way of doing things. So they set out to make the church safe in their own way. Creeds and theologies protected it from individual vagaries; riches and power against outside attacks. The church was safe. But one thing its ardent builders and defenders failed to see. Nothing that lives can be safe. Life means danger. The more the church was hedged about with Confessions of Faith and defended by the mighty of the earth, the feebler it grew."[23]

The great temptation of all religious leaders is to build a system of beliefs or rules which serve as tests of a person's relationship with God and thus a way of determining who is saved and who is going to Hell. But that error draws us away from what God has been trying to do for humanity. Instead, it puts the emphasis on what we must do to please God.

Fortunately, some early Christian theologians avoided this error as they developed ways of thinking about what God was doing in the life, teaching, death, and resurrection of Jesus Christ.

For example, Irenaeus, one of the early church leaders who lived in the second century after Jesus' death, developed an understanding of God's saving work which said that Jesus was the Second Adam and that, as such, he went through all the stages of the First Adam except that Jesus did not succumb to the devil's temptation. Jesus recapitulates or "goes over the same ground" of Adam, but with opposite results. In this case, Jesus wins the battle with the devil in contrast to Adam who lost the battle and, therefore, he assures us that the power of the devil over our lives has been broken. For Irenaeus, it was not just the individual whom the Christ saved by defeating the devil but humanity as a whole.

A little later, Origen, another early church leader, developed Irenaeus' thought further by offering what has been called "The Ransom Theory." Origen taught that God offered the Christ as a ransom to the devil to obtain humanity's release from bondage. The devil accepted the ransom, not knowing who Jesus was. But once he had Jesus in his possession, the devil found the presence of the sinless Jesus intolerable and was forced to let him go.

These two theories or explanations of the work of Christ on the Cross held sway with some modifications and additions for over nine hundred years in the church. Although they may sound quaint and antiquated to our ears, they spoke forcefully to the people of that time frame. And when we examine them, we may find that they still have something to say to us today.

For one thing, they remind us that any individualistic understanding of God's saving activity is incomplete. Dr. Robert Paul speaks to this point in his 1960 book *The Atonement and the Sacraments*:

> A theological liberal living in an age of individualism might very well reject this as an impossible conception of redemption, but most people today have been born into a world that has become thoroughly disillusioned with individualism, and in which the old false securities, upon which the nineteenth century's supreme confidence in individual man were based, have been swept away. The world of concentration camps and atomic power, of technology and totalitarianism, not only brings home to us our solidarity in sin and guilt but also demonstrates that on the level of human society we live or die as a race. Redemption on that level, at any rate, must involve both me and my neighbor, and involves us in reconciliation. It is useless to speak to the member of some small central European or Asiatic country about his democratic freedom of choice and his individual responsibility when he knows

that… its fate, along with his and that of his
children, is entirely in the hands of juggernauts
of world power. He knows that he is involved,
whether he likes it or not, in cosmic ruin or
cosmic salvation. In the face of the world in
which we live… it is surely of some significance
to know that right at the heart of the Christian
gospel is the announcement that God in
Christ has linked his 'destiny' with man for his
redemption.[24]

Both these theories of the atonement remind us of our
solidarity with all other people. They also make us aware of the
forces of evil that constantly attack us and threaten to destroy
us. We may not believe that these evil forces exist outside our
own minds, and Peter Berger is certainly right when he says,
"The average middle-class American, upon having a vision of a
demon, is more likely to call a psychiatrist than an exorcist."[25]
But does that mean that what the Apostle Paul called
"principalities and powers" do not exist and that we do not
need God's help in overcoming them? There is considerable
evidence, in our individual lives and in the world, of a power
of evil that has an existence of its own – if only as the collective
impact of all of our evil. If this evil exists, we need help from
God in confronting and defeating it. These theologians of long
ago may be calling us to consider one very important aspect of
God's redemption.

In 1931, the Swedish theologian Gustav Aulen wrote a
book *Christus Victor.* In it he reminded us of the relevance of
this often forgotten theory of the atonement. Aulen argued
that we need this understanding of Christ's victory over the

powers of evil so that we can confront the evil of our world with a battle song of triumph, He reminded us of two recurring threads in scripture. The scriptures of ancient Israel portrayed the saving activity of God in human history as a defeating of the dragons of chaos. The New Testament writers used similar imagery when they proclaimed that through Christ's victory on the Cross, "the Prince of this world was cast out," "the great dragon was thrown down," and "the power of him who has death at his command" was "broken." (John 12:31; Revelation 12:9; Hebrews 2:14)

These scriptural images may sound fanciful and odd until we remember how the movie *Star Wars* and its sequels have captured the imagination of millions with their portrayal of the battle between good and evil and their secular benediction, "May the Force be with you." Or think about the huge popularity of J. R. R. Tolkien's *Lord of the Rings* with its battle scenes in which Frodo and his band struggle against the forces of darkness and destruction. We need to know that the power of good is greater than the power of evil, if we are to have the courage to continue the struggle for the causes that hold back the tide of evil and that give us hope for a day when truth and justice and love will prevail. This is the hope that has kept people singing, "We shall overcome… some day."

And this hope enables individuals to continue their struggle to defeat the forces that have taken them captive and made them slaves. In his book *Atonement and Psychotherapy,* Don Browning says that in his counseling, the claim of the victorious Christ is the most helpful understanding of God's saving activity to his clients. People who feel powerless before the dark forces ruining their lives find liberating news in the assertion that they have an ally in their battle. Whether it is alcohol or fear or hopelessness or some other darkness that consumes them, the oppressed find hope in knowing that God in Christ has already defeated the powers that threaten them. Browning says, "The process of change suggested by psychotherapy has been best symbolized in the history of Christian thought under the rubric of 'battle and victory.' Irenaeus' *Christus Victor* motif captures the essence of this struggle."[26]

I will return in a moment to the psychological insights which help us understand how God's saving activity rescues us from many present-day Hells. But let me first go back in history to introduce a man who developed a theory of the atonement which has never received the attention which it deserves.

Peter Abelard was a contemporary of Anselm's, but his understanding of what God was doing in Christ was far different. Abelard believed that human beings needed to be changed, not God. It was not God's honor or justice that needed to be satisfied. It was human beings who had become estranged from God and who needed to be drawn back to their Creator. How could this be accomplished? Simply put, Abelard believed that the power of God's love poured out on the Cross would "kindle" a response in human beings that would enable them to return their Creator's love. Paul Fiddes describes it this way, "As God was moved to create human beings in the first place because he [*sic*] is love, planting within them his image which is chiefly characterized by love, so he was moved by love to restore them when they broke the bonds of love that joined them to him."[27] When God demonstrates love, humans recognize who they are and to whom they belong; they long to return to the embrace of Divine Love. That demonstration is provided in the life, teachings, death, and resurrection of Jesus Christ.

Another author, James Carroll, claims that Abelard is not showing us how God saves us. Rather, God is showing us in Jesus Christ how we are already saved. He says, "The story Jesus himself told, that of the Prodigal Son, describes a father whose attitude toward his incorrigible son is one of constant love... The son's return home is the occasion not for his redemption, but for his recognition that, in his father's eyes, he was never *not* redeemed... The cross is an epiphany of the permanent and preexisting love of God that needs nothing from the beloved except existence."[28]

Unfortunately, Abelard's understanding of salvation failed to capture the imagination of the church of his day. However, in more recent times, its value has been rediscovered by many. It has served as a bridge or door to new ways of grasping what God was doing in Christ to save us from all sorts of personal and corporate Hells.

Let me give you two examples.

We live in a time when many people look to psychology rather than religion for help with deep personal problems, including deep feelings of guilt and a sense of meaninglessness and despair. People turn to psychology because it offers practical help in addressing some basic human needs. However, some psychiatrists and psychologists who are also trained as theologians have found that what God did in Christ's death and resurrection offers a more powerful answer to those needs than anything the counselor can offer.

Reuel Howe is one of those psychiatrist/theologians. He sees acceptance as the basic need of human beings. He defines acceptance as a relationship of such security that we can expose our most unlovable selves without fear of rejection. The success of the counselor comes primarily from the fact that he/she is an accepting person who allows clients the freedom to express and explore feelings and thoughts that they would not feel safe expressing elsewhere.

David Everett Roberts agrees with Howe when he asks, "Why does psychotherapy work?" He goes on to answer his own question: "The simplest answer is that it provides a situation in which a person can be completely honest with himself (or herself) and with another human being. Conversely, it provides a situation in which he can discover how much he has deceived himself hitherto; the manner in which his ideal picture of himself, his unrecognized needs, and his special way of trying to make the universe conform to his private demands, has caused him to distort reality."[29]

The therapist offers the acceptance that we so desperately need in order to deal constructively with those distortions in our thinking that are causing us such great pain. But Howe believes that the therapist is always an imperfect conveyor of acceptance and the Christian faith offers something more. It offers a perfect and transcendent source of love/acceptance that Howe believes was demonstrated beyond doubt on the Cross. Howe expresses this conviction in these words:

> The only place we can see love that has the power to love the unlovable in his moment of greatest unlovableness is the love that we see on the Cross. And what do we see there? We see love suffering. It is more than just the suffering of a dying man; pure love is suffering the awful burden and pain of the unlovable. It is loving to the uttermost, and for a moment following the suffering, the agony of loving the

unlovable brings extinction – death. Love dies
in the process of swallowing up, absorbing,
taking unto itself that which is its opposite
– unlovableness. This is the kind of demand
that unlovableness makes of love... Just as
trust must contend against mistrust, so love
must contend against hate. The final struggle
between them took place on the Cross. The
Resurrection is the victory of the love of Christ
on the other side of the struggle with the hate
of men.[30]

Howe has expressed the intent of Abelard's teaching in a
way that people familiar with psychological language can
understand.

Don Browning, another psychiatrist/theologian, suggests a
different way of looking at the human problem – the Hells that
we create for ourselves and others – and the Christian answer
from the Cross. He suggests that the human problem stems
from the fact that in an effort to establish our own worth, we
have absolutized finite values. Put more simply, we find our
worth and value in pleasing others and accepting their values.
Out of fear of rejection, we go on trying to build our sense
of self-worth on our ability to please significant persons in
our lives. That means that there are conditions to our worth.
Therefore, we are always on the edge of rejection. In Browning's
view these finite values tyrannize us. They hold us in bondage.
What is more, these evil forces, these conditions of worth that
hold us captive, are not something that we can escape by an act
of willpower. Browning says,

In a sense, the conditions of worth... contain a power of their own, but this power is not independent or self-derived. The power of the self's conditions of worth is parasitic and derived from a source more fundamental than themselves. They gain their power by "robbing" or "diverting" energy from the deeper actualization tendencies of the organism... The point is that both Irenaeus' concept of the devil and the psychotherapeutically derived conditions of worth constitutes real "powers" from which man needs to be "freed" if he is to be saved.[31]

Browning combines the insights of Irenaeus and Abelard. He recognizes our bondage to forces that have power over our lives. He asserts that those powers can best be conquered by the accepting love of God demonstrated in Christ's death on the Cross. He believes that the therapist can offer a partial salvation through what he calls empathic acceptance but, like Howe, he knows that human acceptance is always partial and therefore incomplete. What the Christian faith offers is the perfect acceptance of God's love, demonstrated irrefutably in the death and resurrection of the Christ. This complete and unconditional love of God breaks the tyranny of our self-imposed conditions of worth and enables us to get on with building a life that is full and free.

As we explore all of these concepts of salvation, it is well to keep in mind that the root of the English word "salvation" comes from "salve" – a healing ointment. Salvation, then, is about healing. Rita Nakashima Brock in her book *Journeys*

By Heart joins other feminist theologians in calling us back to this root meaning of salvation. She challenges Western theology which has followed Anselm, who built on the ideas of Augustine, in identifying the human problem with original sin. Brock writes, "While feminists are not naïve about human evil and suffering, we understand sin as historically and socially produced, which requires us to take responsibility for understanding and stopping oppression and suffering."[32]

Brock goes on to define sin as "neither a state that comes inevitably with birth nor something that permeates all human existence, but a symptom of the unavoidably relational nature of human existence through which we come to be damaged and damage others... Sin is a sign of our broken-heartedness, of how damaged we are, not of how evil, willfully disobedient, and culpable we are... *Sin is not something to be punished, but something to be healed*" (emphasis mine).[33]

As I read her definition of sin, I thought back to two books. One of these books illustrates vividly the old way of thinking about sin and salvation; the other book contains a story that portrays very beautifully the way of salvation to which Brock points.

The first book tells the story of Karen Armstrong's experience in a convent where she was preparing to be a nun. In a chapter entitled, "The Death I Have to Die," Armstrong says, "When I walked through the door of the Noviceship the first thing I saw was a text on the wall, the saying of a saint: 'I would grind myself to powder if by doing so I could accomplish God's will'."[34] During the two-year period of training that she had undertaken, she had to be willing to let her self-love and her own will crumble away until it became a little heap of powder that God could refashion.

Armstrong tried valiantly to change herself. She tried hard to pray, to practice humility, chastity, and all the other disciplines. She tried hard not to need people's love and affection. But she still found herself yearning for it. When she tried to be kind or humble, she found pride welling up within her. She could conform outwardly to the rules of her Order, but inwardly she remained the same worldly person, full of herself. She remembered that the theologians had said that Hell is not really a pit filled with fire. Rather, "It is far more terrible than that. It is the endurance of oneself forever and ever with no alleviation at all. You've chosen yourself instead of God, so God gives you yourself. But this time without anything or anyone to distract you. Just you on your own."[35]

Contrast Armstrong's experience with a story told by Rachel Naomi Remen. Remen went every Friday afternoon after school to her grandfather's house. There they had tea together. After tea, her grandfather would light two candles and have a word with God in Hebrew. When the prayers had ended, he called Remen to stand in front of him. As the little girl stood there, the old man would place his hand lightly on her head and begin to thank God for this child and for making him her grandfather.

Remen describes her grandfather's prayers; "He would specifically mention my struggles during the week and tell God something about me that was true. Each week I would wait to find out what that was. If I had made mistakes during the week, he would mention my honesty in telling the truth. If I had failed, he would appreciate how hard I had tried. Then he would give me his blessing and ask the long-ago women I knew from his many stories – Sarah, Rachel, Rebekah, and Leah – to watch over me."[36]

Remen found that afternoon with her grandfather to be a great blessing because it stood in such contrast to the attitude in her own home. Her parents were professional people who valued learning and achieving. There was no praise there. If she brought home a 98 on a report card, her father wanted to know what she had missed on the test. At home she was driven to succeed. But in her grandfather's presence she felt safe and secure. For him, she was already enough. She sensed that when she was with him. He had looked at her as no one else had and had called her by a special name, "Neshume-le," which means "beloved little soul."

Remen's grandfather died when she was seven. She wondered if she would still feel his blessing resting upon her. Could she internalize that blessing? She could, for she says, "Slowly over time I came to understand that in some mysterious way, I had learned to see myself through his eyes. And that once blessed, we are forever blessed."[37]

Through the eyes and thoughts of feminist and liberation theologians, we are beginning to see a much different picture of salvation. We are learning that salvation is not so much a matter of cleaning up our bad behavior and avoiding God's wrath. Rather, it is a matter of getting in touch with our deepest selves, discovering the wounds and hurts that have limited us, and feeling there the healing, empowering love of God that sets us free to be whole and healthy individuals able to challenge the domination systems that enslave us and others.

When we go beyond the limited lens through which we have been conditioned to see God's saving work – the lens provided by Anselm – we discover that theologians and biblical scholars have given us a whole variety of other ways of thinking about how God works to save us from Hell and make us whole. And we realize that the Hell that most of these thinkers envision is not a future place of torment.

So, in the next chapter, I invite you to consider a different concept of Hell.

5

HELL IN
THE PRESENT TENSE

From what I have said so far, it may seem that I no longer believe in either the existence or the usefulness of Hell. As a place of future, eternal punishment, that would be correct. Marcus Borg is right when he tells us that Paul's concept of justification is not about who is going to Heaven or Hell. He goes on to say, "Here, as in much else, preoccupation with the afterlife has profoundly distorted Christianity."[38] I couldn't agree more!

However, I am convinced that Hell is real. Its reality should be apparent to everyone – we try to ignore it at our peril. Hell is a present reality that we create for ourselves, or for others. By all of our talk of Hell in the future tense, we have obscured the Hells in which we and others find ourselves in this present life. Thus, we have failed to address appropriately and effectively all that makes our lives incomplete, miserable, unhappy, unfulfilled, sad, lonely, destructive – in a word, hellish!

So let's take a look at Hell in the present tense.

Siddhartha Gautama, who was later to be known as the Buddha, was born into a life of wealth and pleasure and raised in a palace where his father sought to shield him from the pain and suffering of the world. One day as he ventured out of the palace, he happened upon an old man who was bent over, leaning on a staff, gray-haired and trembling. That day Siddhartha learned about growing old. On a second excursion beyond the walls of the palace, the young prince encountered a person wracked with pain, and learned of illness and suffering. On a third trip, he saw a corpse and discovered the reality of death.

Thus, according to legend, the Buddha was introduced to the facts of life. Soon he left the palace and spent the rest of his life seeking the enlightenment with which to understand and escape the suffering he had observed.

Unlike the Buddha, Jesus Christ was born neither to the palace nor to wealth but to humble parents and to poverty. He didn't have to learn about pain and suffering because it was all around him. But, like the Buddha, Jesus saw his life's task as an effort to address the difficulties that people faced and to help them overcome the pain and suffering that were a part of their lives. As I have already noted, Jesus summed up his mission in the words of the Prophet Isaiah. He was to bring good news to the poor, to proclaim release to the captives and recovery of sight to the blind, and to let the oppressed go free. He was sent to relieve all that afflicted human beings in this present life.

Scott Peck, a well-known psychologist and prolific writer, begins his book *The Road Less Traveled* with the comment, "Life is difficult."[39] It is Peck's thesis that we cannot deal effectively with life until we accept the fact that life isn't going to be easy. Once we accept the fact that life is difficult, we can get on with addressing those difficulties and finding ways to live life more effectively and joyfully.

These two great religious teachers and the modern psychotherapist agree – life is filled with many things that make us miserable, incomplete, and painful. Only when we recognize their presence can we seek the power and wisdom to do something about them.

In other words, Hell is around us, among us, and within us right here and now. Once we admit that Hell is a present reality, we can work with God to change our society, our world, and ourselves so that the exit gates of Hell are opened and we can start to live as God intended.

When we think of Hell, our tendency is to focus on attitudes and behaviors in our individual lives that create personal havoc and discord. I will return to those in a moment, but it is well to begin where Jesus and the prophets before him began, with the social ills that create a living Hell for a multitude of people. Much of the suffering of the world is not self-inflicted. War, poverty, genocide, torture, slavery, oppression, and displacement all find their roots in a corporate disorder, and the victims often have little control over the Hell in which they find themselves.

The emptying of these Hells is an enormous task. It begins as most tasks begin, with an awakening. For people born in affluence and freedom and shielded from the devastation of war and poverty, as the Buddha was, for example, it is impossible to fathom the pain and suffering which some people endure. We who have never missed a meal cannot feel the hunger pangs of millions who go to bed hungry every night. We who have never heard a bomb explode near us cannot imagine the fear of those who live daily with the sound of gunfire around them.

We who have lived securely in one area of the country for a lifetime cannot know the despair of millions of refugees. It is impossible for us to walk in the shoes of those whose experience is so completely unknown to us.

But in our modern world of global communications, we no longer have the luxury of claiming ignorance. We can wake up to the consequences of our own lifestyle and our failure to demand the kind of changes that promote justice and peace from those in positions of power. Those who worship a God of justice must recognize that God has built into our social structure natural consequences for selfishness and greed and injustice. The world cannot tolerate forever the widening gap between wealthy nations and those who do not have the basic necessities of life. Our wealth and power cannot postpone indefinitely the consequences that await us if we do not amend our ways.

Because most religious leaders have been so concerned about individual salvation and so busy warning people about the horrors of Hell in a future life, they have neglected their prophetic responsibility to warn us that God demands justice and care for all of our sisters and brothers on this earth. It is surprising to me that people are so fearful about their eternal destiny, and yet fail to take seriously the biblical message that our failure to love justice and to show compassion will have dire consequences for us and for the society in which we live.

As you might imagine, I have always had an aversion to "fire and brimstone" preaching. However, I am becoming more and more convinced that "fire and brimstone" preaching does have its place. It is needed, not to warn us about the fires of Hell in the future, but to warn us about the fiery devastation that awaits an opulent, affluent society that puts its trust in material possessions and in military might while ignoring the plight of the great majority of the world. The prophets of the Old Testament, who spoke for God to the people, were keen observers of social ills that were readily apparent to those who had eyes to see. The prophets saw in these inequities the seeds of the destruction of the nation. They warned the king and his advisers that terrible things would happen if the people continued to ignore God's demands for justice and compassion.

To take just one example, God said to the Prophet Jeremiah, "I am now making my words in your mouth a fire, and this people wood, and the fire will devour them." (Jeremiah 5:14b) But the prophet's voice was ignored or scorned. The court-appointed prophets, the royal counselors, told the king and the people that everything was all right. The in-house advisors kept saying to the ruler and to the people that they were doing just fine. They had peace. All was well. But Jeremiah knew better. He said, "From prophet to priest, everyone deals falsely. They have treated the wound of my people carelessly, saying, 'Peace, peace' when there is no peace." (Jeremiah 6:13–14) A short time later, the tiny, morally weakened nation of Israel was invaded and the people carried away into captivity!

Unfortunately, the voices of prophets in the church in America and in other affluent Western societies have suffered a similar fate to that of Jeremiah. The church is often captive to wealthy members who control it and who frown on foolhardy clergy who dare to challenge the tenets of an economy fueled by more and more spending on non-essential goods. The church is also in some places captive to the religious right that equates patriotism and national dominance with the will of God. Rarely are voices raised within the church that speak against the greed that consumes our society. Recently, the President of the United States did admonish corporate executive officers and company leaders for excessive greed that has caused havoc on Wall Street. However, he said nothing about the excessive consumption of a whole host of products by the American public that depletes our environment and contributes to poverty and instability in third world countries. Indeed, after the September 11, 2001 attacks on New York and Washington, he urged citizens to go out and spend even more on consumer goods. With the President's lead, most churches have been tragically silent in a time of national and world economic imbalance and environmental crisis.

So for the most part, an awakening to the Hell in which so many people already live, and the Hell that awaits us if we continue on our present path as a society and nation, will have to come from laypeople and a few courageous leaders. There is in all the major religions a consistent demand for justice, for caring for the less fortunate, for love and compassion, and for peace among neighbors and those who interact with each other. A rediscovery of the biblical emphasis on those things that promote peace is the starting place for those who would open the gates for those who suffer the Hell of poverty or war or displacement.

Those who are captured by the biblical vision of peace will discover that it involves more than just the absence of strife. *Shalom*, the biblical term for peace, is an active word. Its core meaning is wholeness, health, and security. But it does not point primarily to an individual's tranquility in the midst of external turbulence. Rather, shalom is a particular state of social existence. It is a state where the claims and needs of all are satisfied, where there is a relationship of communion between God and human beings and nature that leads to the fulfillment for all creation. Over all, shalom describes an active relationship between and among people, a positive involvement with others.

It is interesting to note that there is a similar word to shalom in Arabic. The word *salaam* comes from the same root, and means submission to God – and by extension peace with all creation. A Muslim, then, is one who submits to God and in so doing is called to create the conditions that lead to peace for humanity and the world that we inhabit.

Because both shalom and salaam involve our relationship with each other and the world around us, it becomes apparent that peace with God is impossible for those who fail to work for peace with and for their neighbor. We are all God's children and God holds us responsible for creating the kind of society and world in which all people are treated fairly, all people have the basic necessities of life, all people have a place to live, all people can receive an education, and all people can live in freedom and without fear. That is a big task. It will require courage and wisdom. But God promises to be with those who are peacemakers – not to shield them from harm, but to encourage and sustain them in their efforts.

All the signs warn that we who live in luxury and relative security and freedom cannot escape forever the Hell of conflict and bloodshed that engulfs those in so many other places, unless we take stock of how we have contributed to the systems that afflict our brothers and sisters, and change our ways. Convincing us to seek justice, to live more simply, and to share our resources is the work of prophet and peacemakers. They are our hope to escape the judgment of God.

So Hell is a present **social reality** from which God helps us to escape if we are willing to do those things that make for peace.

But Hell is also a present **personal reality.** Here again God works with us to extricate us from the pit in which we find ourselves. As we examine these personal Hells, it becomes obvious that some are of our own creation, and some have been imposed upon us.

No one that I know of deliberately sets out to create Hell for himself or herself. Hell is most often something that we slip into rather than something we go looking for. Jesus illustrated this slippery slope to Hell very well in his story of the prodigal son. In that story, the younger son grows restless at home. He goes to his father and asks for his portion of the family inheritance. The boy wants to see the world and do things that he has heard about from others, so he journeys to a far country. There, far from home, he wastes his inheritance while having what he imagines to be a great time. Ultimately he ends up penniless and abandoned by the friends that his money attracted. He is reduced to the menial and degrading job (for a Jew) of feeding pigs. He is miserable, broke, and homesick. He is in Hell. He didn't set out in the beginning to go to Hell. He merely intended to have a good time and savor the freedom of youth – as so many of us would too. But his choices and his actions landed him in a kind of Hell nonetheless.

I know of a very fine, loving mother who wanted very much not to have to work outside the home so that she could be with her children during the early years of their lives. But this mother and her husband bought an expensive house and two big cars and sent their two children to an expensive private school. The mother wanted to stay at home but she also wanted a lifestyle and a status that forced her to keep her job. As the children grew older, the mother suffered the Hell of unresolvable frustration. On the one hand, she wanted to be with her children during their formative years. On the other, she had to work to support the choices that she and her husband had made.

I have met some people who are cranky and disagreeable and critical. Friends and relatives avoid them because they are difficult to be around. These grumpy people are usually lonely, and their loneliness adds to their perception that the world is a terrible place and that other people are no good. I volunteer for an organization that drives elderly people to medical appointments. Some of these elderly people have children living in the city but they have estranged themselves from their offspring by their constant complaining, criticism, and manipulation. These people didn't set out to become disagreeable and unpleasant. They probably drifted into a pattern of behavior that seemed to get results for a while but has long since ceased to gain them what they want and need. They live in a Hell of isolation and loneliness that they have slipped into without even being aware of what is causing their great distress.

The executives who were exposed recently as white-collar criminals probably didn't set out to defraud investors and employees. Most of them were energetic, charismatic businesspersons who had the expertise to build or expand a company and make it very profitable. However, somewhere along the line, they lost sight of their original goal and they got caught up in the allure of wealth and power. At some point they became captive to their own success. They stepped over the line that led to dishonesty and deceit. They now live in a Hell of their own making. Sadly, many of them probably are unaware of, or unwilling to admit to themselves, where they took the wrong turn that led from honest executives to manipulating thieves.

Similarly, those who are caught up in the Hell of various forms of drug addition did not set out to be addicts. Perhaps they were just trying to be popular and go along with the crowd. Or maybe they were trying to escape what they perceived as the Hell of loneliness or fear when they took their first drink, or cigarette, or joint. Maybe they were under a lot of pressure at work and simply stopped off for a few drinks on the way home. In many cases they were caught up in a culture that glorifies and popularizes drinking or drugs as a necessary social lubricant or an efficient way to cope with anxiety. They became addicts over a period of time. Their Hell of addiction is something that they try desperately to deny. That is why the initial steps of most 12-Step recovery programs require these persons to admit that they are in the grip of a power beyond their control.

The road to the present reality of Hell is rarely a straight highway that we take knowing the destination before we depart. It is more often a winding, twisting path that has many attractions along the way to distract us from our ultimate destination. Like the young man in Jesus' story, we don't purposefully set out to go to Hell. More often than not, we end up there to our great surprise.

It is true that there are always warning signs along the way. They could have given us a clue as to where we were heading. But we are usually oblivious to those warnings. Most of us have to learn things for ourselves rather than learning from the mistakes of others or from those who have previously traveled that road.

When the Creator gave us free will, we were given both a blessing and a curse. We were blessed by the freedom to make choices that make us truly human and not puppets. But we were cursed by the fact that we often do not have enough experience or wisdom at the moment to make wise choices. That means that we often ignore the warning signs or the advice of those who have gone before us and we end up in Hell.

But there is a way out of the Hell that we have created for ourselves, and like the exit from the social Hell, it begins with an awakening. In the story of the prodigal son, Jesus says that this young man "came to himself." He had one of those "aha" moments. It suddenly dawned on him that things were better for his father's hired servants than they were for him in this pigpen.

The story doesn't tell us how long the son labored there in the pigpen stubbornly refusing to admit to himself that he had blown it. If this were a typical young man, he may well have spent several years cursing his situation, blaming his father and older brother and everyone except himself for the Hell in which he found himself. Jesus told a story with a happy ending, but he could have told of a young man who preferred to tend the pigs for the rest of his life rather than admit, to himself and to his father, that he had taken the wrong path.

I'll consider, in a moment, the fate of those who prefer the pain of the present Hell they are experiencing to the pain of self-examination and change. For now, though, I want to stay with the man in Jesus' story. He took a look at his life and he didn't like what he saw. It became clear that he had messed up his life. He had blown his chance at freedom and happiness, and he was willing to admit to his father that he had made some very unwise choices. So, he got up and headed for home.

Actually, that is where all of us have to begin if we are to find a way to escape the Hell in which we find ourselves. The way out of Hell begins with a reality check – with an honest examination of our lives to see what it is that is blocking the happiness and fulfillment that we seek. We have to be willing to admit to ourselves and to others that something is wrong and to seek help in making changes that will set us on a new path.

This is the underlying purpose of the confession during the worship service that many people attend each week. It should be the objective of the period of self-examination that Christians engage in during Lent and Advent. However, the confession we offer in worship is often diffuse and unfocused. It is too often centered on Anselm's theology of how we have displeased a holy God who demands perfection from us. It assumes we can never be good enough to deserve God's commendation and approval. It rarely produces those moments when we catch a glimpse of a behavior or attitude that is hurtful to ourselves or others – an insight into how we have become addicted to power or money or drugs or sex, of how we are losing our ethical moorings. It fails to make us aware of an action or a way of thinking that denies us the happiness or peace we seek in this present life.

That is terribly unfortunate. Because God calls us to confession, not to make us feel unworthy or inadequate as children of the Divine Parent, but so that we can see those things that are keeping us from being all that we were created to be. Like any good parent, God is interested in our development. God cares about those things that prevent us from finding the happiness and fulfillment parents always wish for their children. The purpose of confession is to give us time to take stock of our lives and to find those areas that are out of harmony and that are blocking us from achieving the happiness

God seeks for us. We come to confession or self-examination in order to wake up to that which is making our life miserable.

But awakening is only a beginning. The young man in the pigpen became keenly aware that this was not where he wanted to spend the rest of his life, not where he had intended to be in the first place. Having recognized that fact, he had to act on his new insight. He had to be willing to admit his mistakes, not only to himself but to all those who were affected by what he had done. He had to go back home and face his father and mother, his older brother, and all the members of the family. He had to confess to them that he had squandered a part of the family wealth and had wasted some precious years of his youth. He had to go back and pick up the pieces of his life and begin all over again.

Surely, all this wasn't easy. It is always difficult work taking stock of our lives and determining where things are not the way we want them to be. It is even more difficult to admit that we had something to do with what has gone awry. It is much easier to blame someone else than it is to take responsibility for our own actions or thoughts. I'm sure it wasn't easy for the young man in Jesus' story, and we need to be aware that it won't be easy for us to act on the insights that self-examination have provided.

It won't be easy but it can be done. I have always felt that the prodigal son had the courage to take that first step because he had never forgotten the love of his father — a love which he had experienced while he was growing up, a love that was visible as he left home that day and saw tears in his father's eyes. It was recognition of that love which enabled this young man to take the action necessary to set him back on the track that would lead to what he really wanted out of life.

When he finally finished the long trek back home, he discovered that he was right about the father's love. It provided the power to start anew, to rearrange the priorities of his life, to give him new direction and purpose for living. He had rehearsed his confession speech many times on the way home, but the father cut his words short with a welcome that demonstrated his continuing love, and in that love the boy found a new life.

What that young man found is what Jesus demonstrated as the very nature of God – a love so great that we can have the courage to go through the painful process of changing attitudes, priorities, behaviors, prejudices, desires, addictions, whatever it is that is destroying our lives or preventing us from being fully the person we were created to be. Without the support of this kind of unconditional love and acceptance, we find it difficult to admit to ourselves that we are doing something that is destructive, and we find it impossible to change. With this kind of love, change becomes a possibility.

Some people find this love in their family or from friends or from a counselor, pastor, priest, or rabbi. However, all human love has its limits. Parents can be abusive rather than nurturing. Friends can desert and wound us. Counselors and clergy can betray their calling and hurt rather than heal. It is crucial, then, to discover the gift and power of the steadfast love of God that can never be doubted. That is why it is so important that the church move beyond its portrayal of God as Anselm's harsh and punitive judge to a more accurate picture of God as loving parent or friend. This is why we need to see Jesus' death on the Cross not as a payment or sacrifice to God, but rather as the demonstration of the limitless love of God. This love gives us the power to change and to escape the Hell in which we find ourselves at any given moment.

This is not just an abstract concept, unrelated to daily living. It has immediate practical applications. For far too long, the church, society, and parents have relied on fear as the chief deterrent to destructive behavior and the motivator for change. The church has threatened people with the fires of a future, everlasting Hell. Society has threatened people with jail or even execution. Parents have threatened children with corporal punishment if they misbehave.

Inevitably, if we worship a punitive God, we will model punitive behavior ourselves. Parents who scream at their kids, smack them, spank them, or lock them up, may speak about a loving God, but they imitate a father-knows-best God who expects and demands obedience, and who punishes disobedience. By contract, those parents who genuinely perceive a God of infinite and unconditional love will reveal their relationship with infinite patience and gentle acceptance of their wayward offspring's foibles.

Fear as a deterrent rarely stops destructive attitudes or actions. In some cases, it may produce compliance for a while, but it rarely brings about genuine change in the individual. We need jails to protect society from those who have harmed others and are a threat to other people. We also need jails where we can demonstrate that there are consequences to breaking the rules of society. But it must be obvious that punishment alone with no effort at rehabilitation is an ineffective tool for preventing crime, and is even less effective in causing people to change their lives. Gandhi once said that change brought about by fear lasts only as long as the fear lasts.

The fear of Hell simply doesn't work in most cases in preventing people from doing what is forbidden. This was illustrated very forcefully in a recent movie called *Road to Perdition*. In the movie, a Mafia boss played by Paul Newman kneels in a Roman Catholic church even as he plans the death of Tom Hanks. Hanks plays the part of a hit man who is like a son to Newman. Newman has already said to Hanks that neither of them will make it to Heaven, but obviously the fear of Hell which he has learned from the church is not sufficient to stop his plans and certainly not enough to cause him to give up his way of life.

Since fear has been demonstrated to be such a poor and ineffective deterrent and change agent, it is time that the church leads the way by pointing to the message which stands at the heart of scripture. There is a power in God's love that calls us to take stock of our lives, gives us the courage to make the changes that will address the discord, pain and suffering which we experience, and restores our lives to harmony and peace.

Those who have been through the Alcoholic Anonymous program have learned that they have an ally in their struggle with the Hell of addiction. Most find that it is only when they admit that they have a problem they cannot solve by themselves that they are ready to seek help from a power greater than themselves. When that realization finally sinks in, they discover that there is a power available which can aid them in their struggle and that there is a way out of the Hell that has been consuming their lives.

The same holds true for all the other Hells in which we find ourselves. The power to detect and to confront the destructive forces at work in our lives comes ultimately from an unconditional love that can be found only in God. When we know that we are loved with no conditions attached, we find the courage and insight to examine what we are doing and to change that which is counterproductive.

An interesting story in the Gospel of Luke illustrates the power of love to expose a corrupt life and to bring about a dramatic change. The story tells of a man who wanted to see Jesus as Jesus was passing through his village. Because the man was short, he climbed a Sycamore tree to get a better view of the itinerant preacher whose fame had spread through the region. When Jesus got to the Sycamore tree, he looked up and said to the little man clinging to the tree limb, "Zacchaeus, hurry and come down; for I must stay at your house today." (Luke 19:1–10)

It was an extraordinary invitation. It must have shocked those who heard it because they knew that Zacchaeus was a tax collector. He collaborated with the Roman army of occupation, collecting taxes from his own people. And furthermore, he collected more money than he turned over to his bosses. In other words, he was lining his own pockets by defrauding his own people. No wonder when the crowd saw Jesus going off to eat with Zacchaeus, they grumbled because this holy man had gone to eat with one they considered to be a sinner.

With the jeers of the crowd ringing in his ears, Zacchaeus took Jesus to his house that day. Here was a prophet, a holy man, who didn't seem to care what others thought of him. That kind of unconditional love opened both Zacchaeus' mind and his heart. He saw that what he was doing was wrong and he found the courage and strength to change, to turn his life around and head in another direction. We don't know how long they talked or what Jesus said. Maybe Jesus didn't say anything. Maybe he just shared a meal with this little man. But, at some point during that visit, Zacchaeus "came to himself" and he didn't like what he saw. He turned to Jesus and said, "Look, half of my possessions, Lord, I will give to the poor; and if I have defrauded anyone of anything, I will pay back four times as much." Love had worked its miracle – Zacchaeus' life was never the same.

So far, I have not heard of a similar miracle among the company executives who recently defrauded a host of people of millions of dollars and cost their employees their jobs. Fear of imprisonment or punishment did not produce either confession or voluntary restitution. That, I believe, is predictable. Tragically, many of these men and women are Christians. Yet for some reason they have not encountered the unconditional love of Christ which could help them take a long, hard look at where they took the wrong path and show them the way out of the Hell that they have created for themselves.

Even more tragically, so few of us are introduced in our Christian experience to a love that is great enough to give us the insight and courage to change whatever needs changing in our lives. The church has been so busy telling people how to avoid a fiery furnace in the future that it has failed to lead people into an encounter with God's unconditional love that can redeem the present moment. The primary task of the Christian church, and of all religions, is to make God's transforming love so real that we see ourselves clearly and long for the life of harmony and peace and justice that makes our individual and corporate life whole.

Peter De Vries captured the essence of this message in a moving novel called *The Blood of the Lamb*. He tells the story of a family whose little daughter was slowly dying of leukemia. One evening, when the father came to the hospital, the young girl was excited because she had just seen an old Laurel and Hardy movie on TV. She said to her father, "The neatest part was when the little man threw a pie in the face of the big man.

I was really scared because I didn't know what that big man was going to do. But guess what? He did not hit back! He waited the longest time and then deliberately began to wipe the custard from his eyes and cheeks and sling it on the floor. It was amazing. The big man just stood there and took it and did not hit back."

A few days after this exchange, the little girl's birthday came around, and the housekeeper decorated a very special cake and gave it to the father to take to his daughter. There was a Roman Catholic church between the parking lot and the hospital, and so as he often did, the father stopped in on his way to pray. That morning, as he rose to leave, he encountered one of the nurses from his daughter's floor. She whispered anxiously, "Did you get the message?"

The father said, "No, what message?"

"It's about Carol," the nurse said. "A terrible staph infection is sweeping the whole floor. The children's resistance is so low. You had better get up there."

The father dashed out immediately, forgetting the cake. But within hours, his little daughter was gone.

After signing the necessary papers, he staggered out of the hospital past the church toward his car when he remembered the birthday cake. He went in, and there it was, just as he had left it. Somehow, as he looked at it, untouched with that precious name on it, it seemed to symbolize all the absurdity and tragedy of an innocent child having to suffer so, and then die! As he stumbled out of the sanctuary, almost blinded by scalding tears, he passed a statue of Christ hanging on the Cross. In a moment of impulsive rage, he took the cake and heaved it straight into that face, the cake and icing hitting just under the crown of thorns.

A spirit of panic swept over him. "What have I done?" he gasped. "What sort of blasphemy have I committed?"

But then, through his tears, it seemed as if the figure on the Cross slowly extricated his hands from the nails and then slowly began to wipe the icing from his cheeks and sling it to the ground. As the father looked more closely, instead of there being anger or rage on that besmeared face, he was almost positive he saw tears in those eyes and running down those cheeks – as if the event that had broken the father's heart was also breaking the heart of this one who represented the love of God. There would be no retaliation, only sympathy and love. And in that moment the man learned something about God that helped in the healing of his own grief and anger.

De Vries tells a fictional story. The Gospel of Luke tells us a true story, with a matching message. As Jesus was being crucified, he looked down at the crowd that had gathered to gawk at the spectacle and said, "Father, forgive them for they know not what they do." (Luke 23:34) As Jesus died, he felt no spirit of retaliation, only love and forgiveness for those who could not see what they were doing. He was not concerned about this affront to God's representative, only about the blindness that turned a group of people into a mob howling for blood.

As I have talked in this chapter about the present reality of Hell, you have probably noticed that I have not used the word "sin" at all. Once again, it is not that I do not believe in sin. I have avoided the word because it has been so overused by evangelists who often speak of Hell as the eternal punishment for our sins. When they talk of sin, they are usually concerned with the plural use of the word. They warn us against "sins" which can lead us to Hell – usually sexual sins. If they use the word in the singular, they are almost always referring to our refusal to believe a particular doctrine, especially that Jesus was the Son of God and that he died for our sins.

I, too, believe in sin, but it has a much different meaning for me. I believe that the Bible pictures sin as our alienation from the Source of our being and from our own true nature. The Apostle Paul never spoke of "sins." Instead he saw acts of sin as an expression of a deeper problem – the estrangement of the human race from their Creator. The solution, then, lies not in ceasing to do certain things that are considered sinful, but rather, in a new awareness of our Creator's love. Recognizing that love enlists us in the task of reshaping our lives and offering ourselves as agents in addressing the needs of the world. We take on the suffering of the world because God has taken on our suffering. Individually and corporately we find the way out of the Hell that our alienation has created.

Now, I need to return to two threads I left dangling earlier. For those of us who create our own Hells, waking up to what we are doing can start the process of finding the love that makes a new life possible. But what about those whose Hell is caused by others? What about the abused child, the battered wife or husband, the lonely elderly person, the person wracked with pain, or the person who is the object of prejudice or hatred? Is there a way out of the Hell in which these and many others find themselves?

Yes, and it, too, begins with awareness – in this case, the awareness that they are not responsible for the Hell in which they find themselves. Far too often, people blame themselves for the pain and suffering which they experience. Their healing begins with the realization that they are not the cause of their afflictions. Like the child who feels responsible for the divorce of his or her parents, these people need to absolve themselves of blame, find ways to pick up the pieces of their lives, and move on to a healthier life. People who are ill and in pain need to see that illness is not a punishment from God, and need to quit blaming themselves for the pain they suffer. People who are the victims of prejudice need to know they have not been singled out for any intrinsic fault of their own, but rather that their persecutors are filled with hatred.

The way out of Hell for these people begins with awareness but, in most cases, it also involves the help of others in the community. Recovery from abuse and battering often requires community resources and the support of family and friends. The elimination, or at least the curbing, of prejudice and hatred is a communal responsibility. Dealing with pain and suffering can also be made more bearable by caregivers and by organizations such as Hospice. Institutions that are dedicated to caring for those who have no caregivers must address the loneliness of those who have outlived their relatives and friends.

Unfortunately, we as a community often fail those whose lives are a living Hell. We need to be reminded again and again that God calls us to a ministry of compassion and caring as we become the channels of divine love to those in need.

The second loose thread concerns those people who never wake up to their own acts and attitudes that poison their lives. Or they do know, but refuse to admit that they have fallen prey to desires and addictions that are destroying their happiness. Are they doomed to stay forever in a Hell of their own choosing? C. S. Lewis wrote a fantasy tale called *The Great Divorce* in which he addresses this question. He tells of people in Hell who board a bus that takes them to Heaven. As these people arrive in Heaven, they are greeted by spirits who try to persuade them not to return to Hell.

The narrator in this story talks with a man named George MacDonald. MacDonald explains, "All that are in Hell, choose it. Without that self-choice there would be no Hell. No soul that seriously and constantly desires joy will ever miss it. Those who seek find. To those who knock it is opened."[40]

So, we would suppose that, faced with a choice of Heaven or Hell, all would choose Heaven. But the narrator observes that many people refuse to give up whatever it is that has enslaved them. One by one they get back on the bus for Hell.

One particular woman catches the narrator's attention. He says to MacDonald, "I am troubled, Sir, because that unhappy soul doesn't seem to me to be the sort of soul that ought to be even in danger of damnation. She isn't wicked: she's only a silly, garrulous old woman who has got into a habit of grumbling, and feels that a little kindness, and rest, and change would do her all right."[41]

But MacDonald questions whether the woman is a grumbler or whether she has become a grumble. He points out that there is a difference. He says, "If there is a real woman – even the least trace of one – still there inside her grumbling, it can be brought to life again. If there's one wee spark under those ashes, we'll blow it till the whole pile is red and clear. But if there's nothing but ashes we'll not go on blowing them in our own eyes forever. They must be swept up."[42]

I feel that Lewis is certainly on target when he affirms that no one is in Hell who did not choose Hell for himself or herself. God does not send people to Hell; they choose it for themselves. However, I find troubling this story's implication that God finally gives up on some people and lets them remain in the Hell they choose for themselves. This may be true, and I have often been tempted to say that some people seem so burned up with hatred that they destroy themselves. The fire of their own hatred simply consumes them. In this case, they do not remain in Hell because they literally cease to exist. Death is the end for them.

However, I am inclined to think that both Lewis and I have underestimated God. Certainly, there is no indication in the Bible that God ever gives up on anyone. Quite to the contrary, the message of the Bible is that God has worked tirelessly across the ages to reconcile human beings to their Creator. I see no reason to believe that the effort of God to help us become whole and healthy beings will ever cease.

In fact, Jesus' story of the prodigal son, to which I have referred several times, makes this quite clear. In that story, there are two sons. We've already considered the awakening of the younger son. But there is an older brother in the story who remains quite blind to his alienation and anger. When the father receives the younger son back with open, loving arms, the older brother refuses to come to the party for his brother and complains bitterly about the father never throwing a party for him. He is the dutiful son who stayed at home but never found any joy in the father's house. He was in Heaven but for him it was Hell.

Although he made a choice – he refused to come in – the father went out to him with love, saying, "Son, you had only to ask and I would have thrown a party for you anytime you wished!" The love of God is eternal and it seeks us out both in life and in death.

John Polkinghorne, a British theologian and scientist, comes to this same conclusion when he writes,

If hell is the place where the divine life has been deliberately excluded, then some have thought that its inhabitants will eventually fade away into nothingness, because the divine Spirit has habitually been denied its sustaining work in their lives. There is some persuasiveness in this notion of annihilation... though it would also represent the final creaturely defeat of the divine purpose of love. It is hard to know what to think, just as it is similarly hard to know whether the universalist hope, that in the end and in every life, God's love will always be victorious, implies that though there is, so to speak, a hell, ultimately, it will be found to be empty."[43]

In his poem, *The Hound of Heaven,* Francis Thompson gives us a graphic picture of God's relentless love. Thompson reminds us that we may run from God's love, but in the end that love will catch up to us. And, when that happens, we will know that the One from whom we fled is indeed the One whom we have been seeking in our desperate search for meaning and fulfillment and life. The Hells we create in this life may follow us into the life to come. But God's love also follows us wherever we are and that love will ultimately prevail. In the end, the halls of Hell will be deserted!

6

HEAVEN AS PAST, PRESENT, AND FUTURE

It would be impossible and certainly incomplete to talk about Hell without also looking at Heaven. In ancient cultures the two concepts grew up side by side. Hell was the place where evildoers were punished; Heaven was the place where those whose good deeds outnumbered their bad deeds were rewarded. Heaven, then, became the "carrot" that promised rewards for good behavior or faithfulness to a particular god, just as Hell was the "stick" that warned people that terrible punishment awaited those who offended the gods, those who broke the rules of society, or those who injured their fellow human beings.

The idea of Heaven as a reward certainly rings a bell with all who live in a post September 11th world. Mohamed Atta was sure that Allah would reward him for the death and destruction he caused as he flew Flight 11 into the World Trade Center. On the evening before he boarded that flight, he put on perfume and wrote in a letter about the following day, "It will be the day, God willing, you spend with the women of paradise." Some Palestinian suicide bombers have been recruited with promises that they will go to Heaven and delight in the company of beautiful virgins.

And, lest we think that it is only Muslim visions of the rewards of Heaven that have inspired acts that led to death and destruction, we need to remember that as Pope Urban II sent out his soldiers on the First Crusade, he implied that if they died in battle they would ascend directly to Heaven where they would be with Christ. In that crusade and the others which followed, men fighting in the name of Christ wiped out whole villages of Jews as well as Muslims. Their fear of death was tempered by the fact that they had been promised the glorious rewards of Heaven if they should die.

And much more recently, Paul Hill, a former Presbyterian minister, was convinced that a Heavenly reward awaited him after his execution on September 3, 2003, for the murder of a doctor who performed abortions. In 1994, Hill gunned down Dr. John Britton and his escort, retired Air Force Lt. Col. James Herman Barrett, outside the Ladies' Center in Pensacola, Florida. Hill had said in a jailhouse interview, "The sooner I am executed... the sooner I am going to heaven... I expect a great reward in heaven. I am looking forward to glory."

Even some Jews have been led by a belief that God rewards holy martyrs to commit atrocities in God's name. In an article entitled, "Sacred Violence: the dark side of God," Gareth Lloyd Jones reports the following incident:

> On 25 February 1994 Dr. Baruch Goldstein,
> an ultra-Orthodox Jew of American extraction,
> entered a mosque in his hometown of Hebron
> in Israeli-Occupied Territory carrying a
> machine gun. Before he was overpowered

and beaten to death, he had shot 29 Muslin worshippers as they knelt in prayer.[44]

We could dismiss this horrible act as the work of a madman, except for the reaction of other Jews to what he had done. Jones goes on to report that Goldstein's grave has been turned into a garden of remembrance. Some Jews now refer to him as a saint. The inscription on his gravestone reads, "Having given his life on behalf of the Jewish people, its Torah and its ancestral homeland, he was an innocent, pure-hearted individual." Some Jews believe that what he did was the will of God and that he has now been received into Heaven with honors.

Christian theologians, Muslim scholars, and Jewish rabbis have all repudiated the idea that those who kill innocent people in the name of Christ or Allah or Jehovah will be rewarded in Heaven. But these extreme examples point out how the reward motif can be misrepresented and manipulated to encourage acts of violence that all three of these great religions have condemned.

In spite of its misuse, the promise of reward or comfort or joy or release from pain and suffering continues to make Heaven a very attractive concept. It is no surprise then, that a *Newsweek* Poll finds 76 percent of Americans believe in Heaven and 71 percent think that it is an actual place. We desperately want to believe that death is not the final chapter of life, so we welcome a concept which assures us that life extends beyond the grave.

But we must avoid the danger of putting too much stock in the life to come. As one devout Christian blurted, "If I didn't believe that there was an everlasting life, this life wouldn't be worth living."

An over-emphasis on life after death prevents us from seeing how Heaven and Earth can be partners rather than rivals. Look with me at the possibility that **it is only in the blending of past, present, and future that our lives are made whole and complete**.

Our hope for the future begins in the past as we become convinced that our world and our lives have meaning and value given by a purposeful and loving Creator. If our world were simply the result of an explosion of great forces that brought into being the universe with no rhyme nor reason behind it, we could only live for the moment and try to make the best out of whatever hand life has dealt us. But, if that Big Bang billions of years ago signaled the beginning of a thoughtfully designed universe brought into being for a purpose, then we have a foundation upon which we can construct our lives and our society. If we have been asked to be co-creators and stewards of our tiny portion of that vast universe, we find both a reason for our existence and our value as persons. We have a part in the great evolutionary process that God has set in motion – a process that extends far out into a future that may or may not include this planet on which we live.

John Polkinghorne makes two points crucial to our understanding of how the creation of the universe, and our own planet earth, inform and sustain our hope for the future.

First, **God includes us in the evolutionary development of creation**. The world as we know it did not spring ready-made and fully formed out of nothing at the snap of the divine fingers. Instead, it developed through the intricate unfolding of physical process, moving from initial simplicity to immense complexity. Polkinghorne writes:

Theologically one can understand this complexity as the result of creation's having been endowed by its Creator with a profound potentiality which it has been allowed to explore and realize as it 'makes itself.' God is not the tyrannical puppeteer of the universe, pulling every string so that all must dance to the divine tune alone, but rather the Creator is the God whose nature of love is patient and subtle, content to achieve the divine purposes in an open and developing way, in which the creatures themselves collaborate.[45]

God has something in mind for us and for creation. But God will not impose that divine plan upon us by force. So, God works tirelessly with us in the continuing unfolding of the world of which we are a part.

And Polkinghorne goes on to point out, secondly, that **our hope for the future lies in the very nature of the God of creation**. He says, "Hope lies in the divine *chesed*, God's steadfast love, and not in some Hellenistic belief in an unchanging realm of ideas or an intrinsic immortality of the human soul."[46] The God who calls us to be creative partners in the evolutionary development of this world is a God of faithful, steadfast love who does not abandon us when we fail in our part of the partnership. God's love for each individual, for all of humanity, and for the whole created order can be counted on because the very nature of God is love. That means that we have a solid, unshakeable foundation upon which to work in the present and to trust in the future.

The foundation of Heaven laid in the past is the prelude to the Heaven that we experience in the present. One of the great deficiencies of Heaven – as we ordinarily think about it – lies in the fact that it is totally future-oriented. Just as any concept of Hell that focuses exclusively on the future can rob Hell of its most basic warning, so any concept of Heaven that looks only to some future state of bliss can fail to motivate us to work for the kind of society that reflects God's Kingdom on this earth.

This is one of the concerns that has caused several theologians ranging from Friedrich Schleiermacher to Paul Tillich to develop a concept of Heaven that is called "realized eschatology." Eschatology is the study of the "last things" or the "end times." In her book, *The End of the World and the Ends of God*, Kathryn Tanner argues that the end of time does not point to a particular time in the future. Rather, there is a continuum of end time that corresponds to the unfolding of God's creative purposes, manifest in the evolutionary process of the universe.

The problem with the traditional view of Heaven as a place of future rewards is that it often ignores God's concern with redeeming and filling the present life with happiness, meaning, and pleasures. Slaves were counseled to be submissive to their owners in the hope of a much different life in heaven where they would be free and their suffering would be ended. Until the recent advent of Liberation Theology, religious leaders have used the promise of Heaven as a way of keeping the impoverished people of the world from rising up to demand justice and from overthrowing the rich and powerful who kept them in economic bondage.

Any understanding of Heaven is incomplete if it fails to see that God desires that the present moment be filled with a sense of the Holy and the presence of God – that we experience joy and laughter; that pain and suffering be diminished; that justice and compassion prevail; that human needs for food, shelter, and clothing be met; that we be surrounded by the companionship and warmth of friends and family; that we have meaningful work to do and outlets for our creative abilities. Jesus said that he had come "that we might have life and have it abundantly." (John 10:10)

The concept of Heaven on earth has deep biblical roots. You may remember from chapter two that the Hebrews did not believe in either Heaven or Hell until just a few centuries before the birth of Jesus. Throughout the Hebrew Bible, the Israelites thought in terms of God's blessings poured out upon a man (women received their blessings through the men) *in this life*. If a man had land, flocks, good health, and a wife who bore him male children, he had already received the ultimate blessings of God.

God showed divine concern for the happiness and well-being of all the Israelites by helping them develop laws that would assure honesty, prohibit lust, stealing, greed, and other behaviors that would disrupt social harmony. God inspired prophets who warned the people that if they ignored these laws, the blessings that those laws had brought would be withheld. God set up ways for people to live in peace and harmony and to find the happiness that the Creator desired for all people. Further, God warned the people that if they departed from those ways and broke their covenant with their Creator, their peace would be interrupted, their lands would be taken from them, their families would be carried into exile, their temple would be destroyed.

Heaven on earth – Heaven in the present moment – is always tenuous. It depends on our cooperation with the Creator, because God will never *force* us to do those things that lead to our own happiness. Like any parent, God wishes peace, prosperity, and rich, full lives for us as individuals and for us as a society, but God has given us free will to choose Heaven or Hell on this earth. Just as God does not send anyone to Hell, so God does not force anyone or any social group to walk the path that leads to Heaven.

But God does make every effort to show us the way to Heaven and to give us the power to walk in that way. For Christians, God's supreme effort is put forth in the life, teachings, death, and resurrection of Jesus Christ. In this God-filled man, we learn that the very nature of God is love and that through those who follow that way of love, God's Kingdom is brought to fruition on this earth. As Jesus began his ministry, Matthew says, he "went throughout Galilee, teaching in their synagogues and proclaiming the good news of the kingdom and curing every disease and every sickness among the people." (Matthew 4:23)

Then Matthew gathers together the essence of Jesus' teaching in what we have come to call "The Sermon on the Mount." (Matthew 5–7) In that sermon, Jesus describes the attitudes and actions that move us toward God's promised kingdom and that bring us the happiness and fulfillment we seek. He says that the poor in spirit, those who mourn, those who are meek, those who hunger and thirst after righteousness, those who are merciful, those who are pure in heart, those who are peacemakers, those who are persecuted for righteousness sake – these will be blessed. These will find the happiness that God's kingdom on earth can produce.

As you look at the Beatitudes and the rest of this sermon, you realize that Jesus is not talking about what you must do to get to Heaven when you die. He is talking about what you must do in order to experience the kingdom right now. "Blessed are the poor in spirit, for theirs is the kingdom of Heaven." Not "theirs *will* be…" but "theirs *is*" the kingdom of Heaven.

Jesus tells us that we can find a foretaste of Heaven in this life. However, he does not simply dangle this possibility before us and then leave us powerless to achieve the happiness that it promises. In his teachings he shows how to find the path to happiness. In his personal reflection of God's compassion and in his willingness to become a servant, we find the true nature of God – a revelation that gives us the motivation and courage to begin the journey down that path to wholeness and life. Finally, in Jesus' death and resurrection, God demonstrates that the power of evil does not have the final say, and so we find confidence to stay on the path and to know that love will ultimately prevail despite all the evidence to the contrary.

Because we believe this, we keep working for justice and peace. Because we believe this, we try to build a society where the weak and poor and powerless are defended and given aid. Because we believe this, we build our lives on compassion and truth and try to reflect these virtues in our relationship with others.

Because we know that our origin is in a purposeful Creator and because we have experienced God's transforming love in Jesus Christ, we find the faith to work with God in making this life more like Heaven.

But there is something else that keeps us on the path. The hope of resurrection promises that what began at creation and continues through this life does not end at death but has a future. "Realized eschatology" is a much-needed correction to a "pie in the sky" faith that ignores the difficulties and the possibilities of this life. It reminds us that God did not create this world simply as a stepping-stone to a life to come. This life has meaning and value in and of itself.

However, having said this, we must also recognize the limitations of realized eschatology. Heaven on earth is never complete, never fully realized. This life is filled with too much difficulty and pain to be the whole story. Some people live long, fruitful lives, but many other lives are cut tragically short. Some people have an abundance of this world's material goods, while others barely eke out a living. Some people live relatively pain free lives, while others are wracked with pain. Some people are blessed with health and competence, while others are severely limited mentally and physically. Surely, a God of justice and mercy and love cannot be satisfied with a human lifespan that is so short, so uneven, so incomplete – even in the best of circumstances. Polkinghorne reminds us, "Without a transcendent future, many are condemned to a loss of good that no process solely within history could ever restore to them. In fact, all of us are so condemned, even if we have the good fortune to die in honored and pious old age. We shall all die with unfinished business and incompleteness in our lives. There must be more to hope for."[47]

But is hope in the life to come simply wishful thinking? If it is, this wishful thinking seems to have been around for a long time. It seems to be practically universal. Mircea Eliade, a highly respected authority on comparative religions, points to evidence that indicates that people living as far back as the time of the Neanderthals believed in survival after death. Corpses were dusted with red ocher which represented a symbol of life. And then she goes on to say, about the possessions buried with the deceased person, "The burials confirm the belief in survival (already indicated by the use of red ocher) and furnish some additional details: burials oriented toward the East, showing an intention to connect the fate of the soul with the course of the sun, hence the hope of a rebirth, that is, of a post-existence in another world; belief in the continuance of a specific activity; certain funeral rites, indicated by offerings of personal adornment and by the remains of meals."[48] Other anthropologists have made similar observations about the burial practices of people in practically every culture and every time frame.

But wishful thinking, even if it is common to all human beings in every age, does not verify that something actually exists. To bolster their desire to confirm that there is a life after death, some people cite the accounts of those who have had "near death experiences." In his bestselling book *Life After Life*, Raymond A. Moody describes the experiences of several people who had been declared "clinically dead" but who survived and were able to tell about a life beyond this life that they were able to glimpse briefly. Typically, these people describe leaving their bodies, traveling through a long dark tunnel, arriving at a place where they are greeted by friends and relatives and embraced by warm spirit, a being of light. After being asked to evaluate their lives, these people all came to a barrier where they discovered that the time of their death had not arrived and they reluctantly returned to earth.

These accounts are comforting. They seem to give us a first-hand glimpse of Heaven. However, even Moody himself warns against jumping to the conclusion that these experiences prove that there is life beyond this earthly existence. He says, "Let me say at the very beginning that, on grounds I will explain much later, I am not trying to prove that there is life after death."[49]

While not completely dismissing these experiences as validations of the existence of life beyond death, theologian Hans Küng notes several arguments that question the conclusions drawn from near death accounts. He points out that not all those who have a near death experience report it as a pleasant experience. In addition, he notes that "phenomena like those described are found not only in experiences of the dying, *but also in other peculiar mental states* (emphasis mine). That is to say, they have by no means a priori to do with 'the beyond,' the 'hereafter' or still less with 'eternal life.'"[50]

Our desire, our need, to believe that life goes on after death cannot be proven by the accounts of those who have had "near death experiences." But some would argue that such proof is not necessary anyway, because the Christian faith has the ultimate proof in the resurrection of Jesus and his appearances to his disciples after his death. Here we have the hard evidence, they say, the physical evidence that should remove all doubt. Christians across the centuries have taken comfort in the biblical claim that in the resurrection of Jesus, God conquered sin and death and opened the gates of Heaven for all who believed in him.

But once again, we must rely on conflicting accounts from people who lived 2,000 years ago. Those accounts can leave us with as many questions as answers. If you look closely at the Easter stories as recorded in the four gospels, you will find that they actually reveal insurmountable discrepancies and inconsistencies. There were no eyewitnesses to the resurrection itself. There is no agreement about the persons to whom Jesus revealed himself after the Resurrection. There is no consensus on the sequence or the locality of these appearances.

If our belief in Heaven and eternal life is dependent upon historically verifiable evidence, we will not find it in the resurrection accounts. Hans Küng writes, "In so far as it is a question of entering into God's eternal life beyond time and space, this is a life that cannot be established by the means and methods of historical research."[51]

We cannot prove by pointing to Jesus' resurrection that Heaven is a fact. In the final analysis, belief is always based upon trust rather than certainty. But reasonable trust is far different from wishful thinking. Our trust is based upon the purposefulness of God revealed in creation, in God's deep concern for justice, peace, and the well-being of all the peoples of the earth, and in the image of God as compassionate parent and suffering servant that we find in Jesus Christ. Our trust is based on the reasonable confidence that the God who called this world and us from non-being into being can also call us from death to life. Our trust is based on the reasonable assumption that the Creator has something more in mind beyond the limits of what we have experienced up to this point.

Heaven, then, is a complete package, not a one-dimensional place of future rewards. It assures us that our origin is in God, that our present life is of great concern to God, and that our future is in God's hands. In this three-dimensional trust, we find the call to reflect God's compassion and justice in an imperfect world. We believe that this is what God intended. And we believe that God's love will be the essential nature of whatever is yet to come.

7

EVIL AND
OUR RESPONSE TO IT

There is no disputing the fact that we live in a world filled with greed, anger, lying, brutality, lust, envy, jealousy, and all sorts of thinking and behaving that lead to misery, suffering, fear, and mistrust. The fact of individual and corporate evil is irrefutable. But the question is why. Why do we so persistently act and think in ways that are hurtful? Why do we choose the path of destruction and death rather than the path of building up and life? The question of evil has intrigued philosophers, theologians, and thinking people for a long time.

Consider – we live in a world that has the capacity to feed all the people of the earth. We would not all eat lavishly, but there is enough food to feed everyone an adequate diet. We live in a world that has the resources to house and clothe everyone. Once again, we are not talking about mansions and closets filled with clothes, but a modest home and sufficient clothing could be provided to everyone. We could educate everyone on this planet, and we could provide adequate health care for every person. Family, marriage, friendship, committed relationships, communities and churches provide the framework in which we can find warmth, caring, nurturing, and the fulfilling of our sexual nature. Music, arts, literature, crafts – all provide outlets for our creative impulses.

When you stop and think about it, you can understand why the Book of Genesis pictures God looking at creation and being well pleased with everything.

In the light of all these possibilities for good, why do we choose evil? Why do we human beings often choose to do things that are painful and destructive both to others and ourselves? There have been many attempts to address that question and many different answers offered. For myself, I find the explanation of the origin of evil found in the third chapter of Genesis helpful. Look at it with me for a moment.

To get to the root of evil as this famous chapter depicts it, we have to go beyond some surface explanations. In this ancient myth, the Creator places an original couple named Adam and Eve in a marvelous Garden where their every need is supplied. They have everything they could wish to eat. The climate is mild, so clothes are unnecessary. Shelter is provided. And they have each other, the animals around them, and the Creator for company. They are in Paradise! However, a sinister creature invades their perfect Garden. The snake suggests to Eve that their present existence is far inferior to what they could enjoy if she and Adam ate of a particular fruit that God has forbidden them to eat. The snake implies that God is holding out on them – the moment they eat of this fruit, they will become as powerful as God. Adam and Eve succumb to the temptation, defy God, and eat the fruit.

The traditional explanation of this story is that evil is the result of willful disobedience of God's divine command. Evil is the result of breaking the law. Evil comes from willfully choosing to do that which is prohibited by God or the laws of society. We sin and thus create disastrous consequences when we turn away from what we know is good and holy.

Sounds like a reasonable explanation, doesn't it? Yet, I believe that it overlooks something crucial. A friend once suggested that when we look for an explanation for why something is as it is, we need to keep asking "why" over and over again until we get to the deepest answer possible. In this case, we need to ask why Adam and Eve fell for the line the tempter used, when they were already living in Paradise.

The answer to this "why" lies in the way the snake approached Eve. The serpent asks, "Did God say, 'You shall not eat from *any* tree in the garden'?"

Eve replies that God has given them the fruit of every tree in the garden except the one in the middle of the garden. To eat of that tree will mean death. Then, the serpent springs the trap. He says, "You will not die; for God knows that when you eat of it your eyes will be opened, *and you will be like God.*" In other words, "God is holding out on you, my friends. God doesn't have your best interests in mind." The serpent planted a seed of doubt in Eve's mind and it eventually produced the mistrust that led to disobedience.

The ancient story paints a masterful picture of the basic human problem that lies behind our destructive attitudes and behavior. We don't actually need a slithering serpent to whisper in our ears. We are born vulnerable and mistrusting. Infants are dependent upon their parents to meet their every need. When even the best of parents fail to meet those needs, the infant is thrown into a crisis of trust. Can these parents really be trusted and is the world into which we were thrust at birth a trustworthy place? Based on this scenario, Erik Erikson, one of the leading figures in the field of psychoanalysis and human development, puts the movement from mistrust to trust as the first developmental task in life. How well we accomplish that task, Erikson says, will determine to a large extent how successful we will be with the other developmental tasks that confront us as we make our way through life.

The problem is that none of us, not even the most well adjusted person, ever learns to trust completely. We are all, at times, wary of the intentions of others, suspicious of the motives of our friends and foes, and unable to trust completely that our emotional and physical needs will be supplied. We swing back and forth like a pendulum. On a continuum from one to ten, our trust level reaches highs of seven or eight at times, only to fall to two or three at other times.

And there is good reason for this. Experience tells us that our primary caregivers are not always trustworthy. Even the best parents occasionally fail us – and some parents give their children ample reason not to trust other human beings. Experience also tells us that friends and classmates and neighbors can hurt us as well as bless us. The world out there is not always a caring place and we learn that our trust can often be betrayed. Experience teaches us further that the church, the institution called into being to be a channel of God's grace and care, can also be a place of conflict, rejection, and abuse. It is not always trustworthy in mirroring the love of God to us.

We even find that there are times when God seems to desert us to our foes, when God fails to provide the comfort and protection that our religious leaders claim will always come from God. We set ourselves up to believe that God will swiftly and surely come to our aid, and when that aid fails to materialize or comes in a form that we do not immediately recognize, we feel forsaken and abandoned by the ultimate Source of security. Thus, the Psalmist who feels deserted by God cries out, "My God, my God, why have you forsaken me? Why are you so far from helping me, from the words of my groaning?" (Psalm 22:1) And we find those same words on the lips of Jesus as he hangs on the Cross and feels utterly rejected by the God who was like a father to him.

Absolute trust is impossible for us as human beings. We can move in the direction of greater trust but we never fully arrive at that destination in this life. And out of our mistrust come fear, anxiety, jealousy, greed, anger, and all the other emotions that tear the fabric of our own lives and the cloth out of which society is woven. Mistrust breeds disharmony and discord so that the security of life is often shattered and we are constantly trying to put the pieces back together again.

I offer this explanation because it seems to me that we have been approaching evil from the wrong direction. Our traditional understanding of evil as disobedience would lead us to believe that it can be conquered simply by making the consequences so painful that people will be deterred from doing wrong. If I know that disruptive, destructive behavior will lead to swift and sure punishment, I will think twice before I break the law. If I know that breaking the moral law or defying God will doom me to eternal punishment in Hell, I may live morally and obey God out of fear of the consequences.

This understanding of evil leads to ever more punitive measures. It provides the backbone for arguments that would apply capital punishment, the ultimate penalty, not just for murder, but also for such crimes as rape, drug dealing, and treason.

However, this approach to evil has been only moderately successful at best. In the past, it applied the death penalty for as little as stealing a loaf of bread. It was so unsuccessful that pickpockets found their best pickings among the crowds gathered to witness public executions!

Fear of punishment may keep people in line so that social groups can function with some degree of success, and it may protect us from our own and others' worst destructive behavior. But fear of the consequences of misbehaving is only a temporary solution at best. Mahatma Gandhi understood the limitations of fear as a deterrent. He said, "What is gained through fear lasts only while fear lasts."

But what if we were to approach the problem of evil from a different angle? If we see the origin of evil coming primarily from mistrust, then we see that our task is not one of imposing stiffer penalties for disobedience but rather one of creating the atmosphere in which trust can be nurtured. That must be the starting point in addressing the evil that pervades our lives and our whole world.

At this point, however, something further must be said. If evil has its primary roots in mistrust, and if mistrust is universal, then surely we have no responsibility for the evil we create or the evil in which we participate. Aren't we off the hook if evil has its origin in something over which we have no control? Have I done to evil what Karl Menninger suggested we have done to sin in his book *Whatever Happened to Sin?* Menninger argues that we have found ways to talk about sin that don't make it sound like sin anymore. We talk about sin as an illness or as a crime or as a product of a dysfunctional society. Am I suggesting a way to think about evil that absolves the individual and society from any sense of guilt because It doesn't sound like evil?

That is not my intention, and it certainly wasn't the intention of those who wrote the sacred texts of the world's great religions. In the Christian tradition, the Genesis story was not recounted again and again to let its listeners off the hook for the sorry state of human affairs and the destructive behavior of individuals. Rather, it was told repeatedly to remind those who heard it of the origin of the human malady so that they could seek help in changing things.

We need to remember that the story of Adam and Eve is not a story without hope. In the story, this mythical couple was told that they would die if they ate of the forbidden fruit. But they didn't die! The story continues, because evil will not have the final say in their lives or the life of the world. Our mistrust of God, of each other, and of the world around us produces havoc and chaos in the social order and in our individual lives. But, the story reminds us, God will prove so trustworthy and God's love will prove so steadfast that each of us can be transformed, and trust can be born again.

Our responsibility is to be open to that transforming love. For some that's easier than for others because the roots of trust have been nurtured by human love that pointed to the ultimate expression of divine love. Unfortunately, as I have argued earlier, the transformation which love accomplishes may have to wait for some until an encounter beyond this life.

In this life, our task is to be more conscious, more aware, of the ways our mistrust leads us and society astray. Where does mistrust cause us to seek power over another person? Or, to look at the flip side, where does mistrust make it impossible for us to reveal our true nature to another person and thus become vulnerable, because that other person would know our weaknesses as well as our strengths? Where does mistrust fuel the fires of greed because we are afraid that we will not have enough if we share what we have with others? Where does mistrust of our sexuality cause us to deny our sexual nature, or try to compensate by being sexually promiscuous, aggressive, or abusive? Mistrust invades every area of our lives. We can begin to address it only when we recognize its existence and begin to see the damage that it causes. The task of religion is to call us to the kind of honesty about ourselves and the world that makes change possible. Some call that moment of recognition repentance, others call it enlightenment, but they both point to the same thing.

In a lecture which he gave to a symposium on "Understanding Evil" at Salado, Texas, in 1987, Scott Peck made an interesting distinction between sin and evil. Peck said, "People get confused about the difference between sin and evil. We are all sinners. However, *all sins are redeemable except the sin of refusing to acknowledge that you can make a sin* (emphasis mine). That is what evil is."[52] Evil, then, is not simply doing something that harms you or others. Rather, it is the refusal to acknowledge that you have sinned. Our destructive acts become evil when we fail to constantly examine our thoughts and actions in order to detect those things in our lives that are harmful to ourselves and others.

At its best, when the religious community comes together in confession, the object is not to make us wallow in our sins and bemoan our miserable condition. Rather, the object is to let us examine our lives and to take ownership of those things in us and in our society that disrupt the harmony and peace of our own lives and the lives of others. Confession demands more than merely a cataloguing of our faults and failures, of the bad things we have done or the good things left undone. It may start there. But it must ultimately look deeper at the mistrust, fear, anger, greed, or whatever else causes us to act and think in destructive ways. It must go below the surface to take a look at our hearts and the shadow side of our being, for it is only at that depth that we find the root of that which keeps us from being whole and healthy. For those who are willing to embark on this journey into the self, there is hope for the kind of enlightenment that prevents sin from turning into monstrous evil.

What I have just said about our need for self-understanding could equally be said about social awareness. Mistrust, greed, and fear infect our social order. They wreak an even greater havoc there than they do in our individual lives. When we think of evil only in terms of individual acts, especially moral lapses, we have severely limited our understanding of evil.

We need, then, to look at corporate or social evil, too. I want to suggest two possible ways of doing that. **We can view corporate evil through the lens of mistrust** just as we have considered the impact of mistrust in our individual lives. **We can also look at corporate evil as an entity in and of itself.** I will return to the second way of looking at social evil, but first consider with me how mistrust corrupts our social relations.

Actually, mistrust pervades every situation where interaction between groups take place – our life in families, in business, in communities, in nations, in religion, and in ethnic groups. Let me give you just a few examples.

Mistrust reveals itself very early on in the family circle. Siblings simply cannot believe that their parents have enough love to include all of the children equally. Repeatedly we hear one child say, "Mother loves you best," or "Daddy likes my brother more than me." Or we observe the squabbles over a piece of cake: "It isn't fair. He got a bigger piece than me." Children vie for their parents' attention because they believe that other siblings are getting more attention. This is obviously an individual problem. But it quickly upsets harmony and the family often becomes a battleground for attention and love. The same mistrust that causes conflict in the early stages of family life often persists as parents and children continue to battle into their later years.

Institutions of all kinds are similarly riddled with mistrust that plays havoc with relationships and productivity. Several years ago a man told me a story that illustrates this well. Bill worked for a large company that had many projects in various stages of completion. When his team finished its project, he was left with nothing to do until the team was assigned a new task. So Bill went to his team leader and asked for permission to assist another team that was having difficulty completing its project on time. The team leader refused his request.

When I asked Bill why his request was denied, he told me that his team leader was afraid that if he allowed a member of his team to assist someone else, it would make the other team leader look good. The other leader might get the next promotion rather than Bill's leader. Both team leaders worked for the same company. You might think that they would both want to do what was best for the company. However, Bill's leader was more concerned about his own future than with the productivity of the company as a whole.

This story is repeated over and over again in every business, educational enterprise, and religious institution. Mistrust leads to so much insecurity that cooperation and teamwork is very difficult. In the fierce competition that exists among businesses, institutions of learning, and religious groups, the seeds of mistrust have prompted dishonesty, deceit, and power struggles that make it difficult for these institutions to achieve their intended goal of serving people.

The suffering and disharmony that results from corporate and institutional mistrust is enormous, but they pale before the disastrous consequences of mistrust between nations. Adlai Stevenson once said that, in the realm of international diplomacy, normal ethical considerations could not be considered. In other words, in dealing with other nations, deceit and deception are acceptable. Diplomats and governments feel that if they tell the truth, another nation will take advantage of them. The consequences of mistrust between leaders of nations is obvious for all to see – conflict, starvation, millions of displaced persons, terrorism, economic exploitation, and the ever present threat of weapons of mass destruction.

The potential for evil that comes from individual mistrust expands exponentially in corporate and institutional settings. It reaches disastrous proportions when nations find it impossible to trust each other. This evil can be curbed to some extent at a local level by laws and rules and the threat of punishment for those who carry their mistrust too far. But few rules apply at the international level, and those few have no way of being enforced. A fair and just and caring society can be created only when corporate mistrust is tempered by a spirit of love and concern for others that overrides the temptation to act solely out of self-interest. Addressing corporate mistrust is an enormous task, but not an impossible one. So, it behooves us to search for ways to make our institutions more aware of the destructive consequences of mistrust and the potential for good in expanded trust.

We can also look at corporate evil as an entity in and of itself. Walter Wink has done us a great service in his trilogy, *Naming the Powers, Unmasking the Powers,* and *Engaging the Powers*. In these three books, Wink has helped us take a look at corporate evil in a new way. He would equate this evil with what the Bible calls "principalities and powers." Contrary to the biblical worldview, though, he contends that these principalities and powers are not supernatural beings from outer space. Instead, they exist within institutions themselves. Wink writes, "My thesis is that what people in the world of the Bible experienced and called 'Principalities and Powers' was real. They were discerning the actual spirituality at the center of the political, economic, and cultural institutions of their day."[53]

The biblical writers were aware that institutions have a spiritual ethos, a power of their own. They knew that that power could become evil or corrupt. They attributed this corrupting influence to demons or devils who resided somewhere in the sky. Wink suggests that a modern, integral worldview sees the evil rising from within rather than coming from without. But the results are the same. These "principalities and powers" play havoc with humanity, they bring about much suffering and death, and they prevent us from becoming what we were created to be. When Wink speaks of "demons," he is talking about "the actual spirituality of systems and structures that have betrayed their divine vocation."[54] He uses the expression "the domination system" to "indicate what happens when an entire network of Powers becomes integrated around idolatrous values."[55]

Wink's contribution to the understanding of corporate evil reminds us of how twisted and malevolent our institutions become when they lose sight of God's intended purpose for them. We do well to heed his warning that any attempt to transform a social system without addressing both its spirituality and its outer form is doomed to failure. He advises us to remember that the Powers were ordained by God for creating a more humane world. Therefore, they must be engaged and redeemed so that they can perform their God-intended purpose.

Evil exists on both an individual and corporate level. There have been many attempts to explain its origin and none is totally successful. However, we do understand evil well enough to recognize that it must be addressed on more than one level. I believe that some antidotes to evil – some ways of curbing evil – work better and are ultimately more effective than others.

Getting rid of the mistrust that lies at the root of evil requires work at two levels. On the one hand, we need to teach ourselves to learn to trust more, to risk making ourselves more vulnerable to others. On the other, we need to learn better how to influence the attitudes of those who treat trust as a weakness to be exploited.

8

SOME IMPLICATIONS
OF A DIFFERENT
UNDERSTANDING
OF HELL

In conclusion, I want to offer three observations.

First, a belief in Hell as a place of future punishment to which God consigns individuals lies at the root of the exclusivity in religions that has caused so much pain and suffering in our world.

Second, there is a still more excellent way to which the Bible points us – a way that goes beyond a dependence upon rewards and punishment to motivate people to love themselves and their neighbors.

Third, if the church were to put its emphasis on this way of mature love and concern for one another, it could offer something very attractive to those who have been repelled by a God who sends people to suffer in Hell for acts of defiance, disobedience, or failure to believe prescribed doctrines and who rewards people who are obedient, subservient, and correct in their beliefs with mansions in the sky.

Let me elaborate on these observations.

Expanding and clarifying our understanding of Hell can be far more than an academic or theological exercise. **It could save our world and us from much of the misery and suffering of religious exclusivity.**

Saving people from Hell is the driving force behind much of the conflict between religions today. Different religions, and factions within each religion, believe they have the only formula, the exclusive way, to relate people to God so that they can escape eternal punishment. Because they believe that wrong beliefs can bring down God's wrath and judgment upon individuals, they also believe that those who lead others astray with false teachings must be silenced or eliminated. If you take Hell as eternal punishment out of the equation, the motive for conflict with those who hold different views of God is greatly diminished.

I wrote in a previous book, *Religious Abuse,* that exclusivity is the most destructive form of abuse because it leads to wars and conflict on a grand scale. Exclusivity is born of the conviction that one's belief system is the only valid way to approach God. It has at its core a deep concern for the eternal destiny of people. The fervor of those who are certain that there is only one way to be worthy of God's love is fueled by a genuine desire to save people from Hell.

This misguided concern for the souls of people has led in the past to the Crusades, the Inquisition, the Holy Wars in Europe, and witch hunts in America. This concern persuaded John Calvin, the 16th-century founder of what eventually became the Presbyterian Church, to consent to the death of

Michael Servitus, a teacher in Geneva, Switzerland, for daring to offer what Calvin thought was a heretical understanding of the Trinity. In order to protect the people of Geneva from this false teaching that could threaten their salvation, Calvin believed that Servitus must be silenced.

At the risk of offending patriotic Americans, I suggest that this same concern has driven Osama bin Laden to train terrorists to attack the United States. Bin Laden believes that America is the great Satan, that it has offended Allah, and even worse, that it is luring people away from a proper reverence for the ways of Allah and thus assuring their eternal damnation. It is hard for us to believe that bin Laden does not have other agendas beyond religious purity in his conflict with the West, but there can be little doubt that he is driven, to a large measure, by his distorted interpretation of Islam as the only true way to avoid the eternal displeasure of God.

Even when we discount other motives that lead to conflict in our world today, it is obvious that religious exclusivity has produced enormous suffering and bloodshed – not only in the past but also in our own time. Hans Küng asks, "Are not the most fanatical and cruel political struggles colored, inspired, and legitimized by religion?"[56] Without a doubt, the answer is yes. And we can go on to say that an overriding concern with Hell as future punishment lies at the root of much of this conflict. What we are fighting over is who has not just the best way, but the *only* way, to avoid the fires of Hell.

But suppose we came to realize that there are no fires of Hell. Suppose we were convinced by scripture and plain reason that God has no interest in Hell as a future concept. What would happen if we came to see that God's concern is that we eliminate or reduce the suffering and injustices that plague our present existence and thus create Hell on earth? What if we came to realize that God has spoken through all of the great religions calling us to love one another and to honor the Creator of all things as a way of moving toward building God's Kingdom on earth as it is in Heaven?

By taking away a major source of the fuel that feeds the conflict between religions, we might find instead a common commandment to love God and our neighbor as ourselves.

So my first observation is that if we turn out the fires of Hell, we will make exclusivity unnecessary. We will have taken a big step toward making our world a safer and more peaceful place to live.

Our next task is to move beyond the carrot-and-stick as a way of motivating behavior. In his first letter to the church at Corinth, the Apostle Paul spoke of various gifts that God had given to the people – the gift of teaching, healing, working miracles, and many others. But, he asks this congregation to go beyond these gifts. He says, "I will show you a still more excellent way." (1 Corinthians 12:31) What he wrote next is one of the better-known passages of scripture. It has been called a hymn to love. It begins, "If I speak in the tongues of mortals and angels, but do not have love, I am a noisy gong or a clanging cymbal…" (1 Corinthians 13:1)

Paul points us to a way that moves beyond using the threat of Hell to change behavior or to mold character. He reminded his readers that Jesus, like all the great religious leaders, offers us a different approach to building character. Let me illustrate what I mean.

In the 25th chapter of Matthew, Jesus tells a parable about the last judgment that, as I have already suggested, has more to do with a present judgment than a future one. Note in this parable that those who are commended and those who are condemned had no idea that the deeds of mercy offered or withheld had anything to do with Jesus and thus with rewards or punishment. Whatever they did – whether they visited the imprisoned or didn't, whether they clothed the naked or didn't, whether they fed the hungry or didn't – they did it without a thought that it was Christ they were serving. So, when Jesus stands before them in person, they ask in surprise, "Lord, when did we do this to *you*?"

It is clear that neither the sheep nor the goats in this story acted as they did with any thought of reward or punishment. For the thoughtless, selfish people who cared only about themselves and had never developed the qualities of compassion and concern, this was tragic. They were totally oblivious of the consequences of their behavior. They were like the man in another of Jesus' parables who kept building bigger and better barns to hold all of his possessions without realizing that there was something more to life than wealth and pleasure and self-indulgence. They had no concept of the solidarity of the human family and how when one person is hurting, the whole family suffers. They acted as isolated individuals whose primary purpose in life was to find pleasure for themselves. It never occurred to them that they had any responsibility for anyone else. For some reason they were so insecure that they had to focus entirely upon themselves and were never able to step outside of themselves to experience what others were feeling or thinking.

That is indeed a tragedy. We need to realize that ultimately it cannot be avoided by threats of punishment. The threat of punishment may cause us to share, grudgingly, a token of what we have, but it does not really change our attitude toward others and ourselves. It may force us to share but it cannot make us generous, compassionate people. The change of heart that Jesus desired cannot be achieved by forcing people to do what is right and good.

This should be obvious when we look at those in Jesus' parable who did feed the hungry, clothe the naked, visit the sick, etc. They were as surprised as their counterparts when they were told that they had earned God's commendation and reward. They were not motivated by a desire to escape punishment and to receive a reward. They acted out of a deep empathy that caused them to respond to the needs of others because they felt what the other person in need was feeling. They knew that if they were hungry, they would like someone to bring them food. They knew that if they were sick, they would like someone to visit them. Because of this empathy, they could respond to the universal command of all religions, "Do unto others as you would have them do unto you." However, they responded not to a command but to something deep within them. They were responding to a love that had been lavished upon them and that set them free to love others and be responsive to their needs.

A friend, Dr. Frederick Ritsch, reminded me in a sermon on this text recently that our task as parents is to move beyond rewards and punishment in instilling values in our children. This preacher was trained in Adlerian parenting skills which teach that if you reward the good and punish the bad, then children will be good in order to be rewarded, and will not be good *for its own sake*. They won't intrinsically adapt the values you are trying to teach them. In fact, if it's all rewards and punishment, then the whole thing could backfire. What you've actually taught them is that *rewards* are good, and *punishment* is bad. Dr. Ritsch went on to say,

> So what happens when the day comes that they realize that doing good might get punished, and doing bad might get rewarded? Studies show that cheating in schools and colleges – not to mention in corporate boardrooms – is on the rise these days. This is in part because students no longer view doing well in school, and having an education, as valuable in and of itself – it is a means to an end, the good grade that gets you the good job.[57]

And so it seems to me that religion has the same task that parents have. We must help people discover this still more excellent way of living. This way of living ultimately moves beyond rewards and punishment and begins to think about the needs of others as well as ourselves. It is a way of living in which we choose truth over falsehood, generosity over greed, love over lust, justice over oppression, peace over war, because these are values that have captured our hearts and minds and control what we think and do.

This cannot be done by coercion or threat. Nor can it be done by insisting on formulas or doctrines that must be accepted in order to find God's pleasure and escape God's wrath. We prepare the way for God's transforming love to work its miracle in people by mirroring God's love and compassion and by patiently waiting for people to discover that kind of love for themselves.

Long, long ago, the prophet Jeremiah foresaw a time when God would enable people to move beyond external laws and to live by an internal law. He speaks for God when he says, "I will put my law within them, and I will write it on their hearts; and I will be their God, and they shall be my people. No longer shall they teach one another, or say to each other, 'Know the Lord,' for they shall all know me, from the least of them to the greatest." (Jeremiah 31:33–34). God longs for the time when we can move beyond laws and rules, beyond reward and punishment, and find our motivation in a deep and abiding faith in God's goodness and love. When that time comes, Heaven and Hell will become obsolete as motivators because we will have discovered the joy of God in the fulfillment that we find in serving others. At the same time, we will discover how that joy fades when we ignore the needs of our brothers and sisters. Our motivation will come from an empathy that is born of God's great love for us, and not from a fear of God's punishment.

Now obviously this is the ideal. Until we can reach the time when people are motivated from within by the power to love to care for each other and not to hurt one another, we will need rules and laws – and the threat of punishment, temporary and ineffective as it has proven to be, to deter and curb evil acts. But the trouble is, we often lose sight of the ideal and think that the threat of punishment can actually produce the results we desire. To lose sight of the ideal is to lose hope. When that happens, we are well on our way to the Hell we are trying to avoid.

If we put out the fires of Hell – if we can drown the fires of Hell with the waters of God's sure and steadfast gracious love – we can remove the pre-eminent reason for exclusivity. We can move toward a kind of motivation that doesn't depend upon the threat of punishment as its chief means of controlling people. And we will do one thing more. We will be able to offer people a vision of God that is magnetic in its appeal.

It is time for the Christian church and all other religions to give the world a clear and unambiguous picture of God as the purposeful Creator, the Covenant Maker whose steadfast love never wavers, the Redeemer who waits patiently until we are ready to be rescued from the Hells that we have created for ourselves. It is time for us to make it clear that there is no Hell to which God sends people for eternal punishment.

We do indeed have "Good News" to share with the world. For far too long, however, we have been turning that good news into very bad news. We have been turning a loving, compassionate God into a vindictive tyrant. It is time to confess that we have misrepresented the God we are called upon to proclaim. **I am convinced that when we are willing to say, without hesitation or equivocation, that the fires of Hell, as they have been preached for so long, do not exist, we will open the door to faith to a multitude of people.**

From the pulpit, in the classroom, and in our individual conversations, we need to correct and repudiate a concept of God that is repugnant. When we do that, I am convinced, we will give our members a new enthusiasm for evangelism, a new enthusiasm for sharing their faith with others. When we discover the power of God to rescue us from the present Hells in which we find ourselves, we will have wonderful good news to share with others. We will then be able to offer people a way out of the personal Hell that enslaves them. And we will have a powerful message that shows the way to eliminate much of the corporate Hell that has set our world ablaze with scandal, anger, misery, and suffering. The time has come to repudiate the Hell Jesus never intended and to rediscover his God of steadfast love and compassion!

A SURVEY OF BELIEFS AND ATTITUDES ABOUT HELL

Hell Survey Tabulation

First ( ) = number out of 104 responses from congregation at large

Second ( ) = number out of 37 responses from seminary students and faculty and Austin area pastors

1. What is Hell?
   A. Separation from God. (76) (26)
   B. A metaphor for God's judgment. (3) (3)
   C. A theological "stick" (i.e., punishment). (3) (0)
   D. An outdated concept. (5) (0)
   E. A lake of fire in which the damned are tormented for eternity. (3) (1)
   F. A present reality from which God offers the power to escape. (15) (7)

2. What is the purpose of Hell?
   A. Eternal Punishment. (27) (8)

B. Refining and purifying leading to reunion with God. (13) (3)

C. Punishing and refining leading to reunion with God. (4) (3)

D. A present awareness that calls us to seek help to overcome the forces that are destroying our life. (52) (18)

E. Serves no useful purpose. (6) (3)

3. Who is going to Hell?
    A. Those who fail to show love and mercy. (31) (6)
    B. Those who fail to care for the poor. (0) (0)
    C. Those who are unjust and unfair. (1) (1)
    D. Those who do not profess their faith in Jesus Christ. (19) (13)
    E. Only the most evil – Hitler, serial killers, etc. (9) (0)
    F. No one. (26) (8)

4. Upon which biblical images do you base your belief in who is going to Hell?
    A. Jesus' story of the rich man and the beggar, Lazarus, found in Luke 16:19–31. The rich man had everything in this life; the beggar was poor and ill. The rich man finds himself in Hell; the beggar ends up in Heaven. (8) (1)
    B. Jesus' picture of the Last Judgment in Matthew 25:31–46. The King in Jesus' story says, "You that are accursed, depart from me into the eternal fire prepared for the devil and his angels; for I was hungry and you gave me no food, I was thirsty and you gave me nothing to drink, I was a stranger and you did not welcome me, naked and you did not give me

clothing, sick and in prison and you did not visit
me." (32) (10)

C. Jesus' description of God's love, in John 3:16, that
"God so loved the world that he sacrificed his only
begotten son" in the familiar words of the Authorized
(King James) Version. (24) (8)

D. Paul's advice to the Philippian jailer, in Acts 16:30–31.
"What must I do to be saved?" the jailer asked. Paul
replied, "Believe in the Lord Jesus and you will be
saved, you and your household." (14)(3)

E. Other: (10) (11)

5. When the biblical writers talk about being saved, what
are we saved from?
A. Hell as a place of future punishment. (16) (7)
B. Ourselves. (20) (8)
C. Things that enslave us – fear, greed, addictive
habits, etc. (39) (12)
D. Loneliness, despair, hopelessness. (13) (3)
E. Meaninglessness. (7) (3)
F. Inability to trust. (2) (2)

6. As you think of your relatives and friends, do you believe
that any of them are going to Hell?
A. Some. (7) (3)
B. None. (30) (5)
C. I would not presume to judge. (64) (29)

7. As you think of your relatives and friends, do you believe that some of them are controlled by forces that make their life "hellish"?
   A. Some. (57) (22)
   B. None. (14) (1)
   C. I am not sure about others, but I have experienced Hell as a present reality in my life. (20) (14)

8. Because it is difficult to think about Hell without thinking about its counterpoint, Heaven, when you think of Heaven, what is the primary image that comes to your mind?
   A. A place where God reigns. (40) (23)
   B. A vision for God's kingdom on earth. (19) (4)
   C. A dwelling place for the deceased faithful. (9) (3)
   D. A metaphor for God's eternal care and compassion. (31) (8)
   E. A theological "carrot" (i.e., a reward). (0) (0)

9. Where did you get your concept of Hell?
   A. From the Bible. (55) (29)
   B. From your parents. (12) (2)
   C. From literature – Dante, Milton. (11) (4)
   D. From TV evangelists. (1) (0)
   E. Have no concept of Hell. (10) (2)

10. **How important do you think discussions** of the afterlife
    are for Christian theology? On a scale of (1–10) in
    which "10" signifies very important and "1" signifies not
    important, rate the theological significance of discussions
    of the afterlife.

    NOT IMPORTANT   VERY IMPORTANT

    1.....   2.....   3.....   4.....   5.....   6.....   7.....   8.....   9.....   10

    (6)   (7)   (7)   (6)   (13)   (7)   (14)   (17)   (8)   (14)
    (1)   (1)   (2)   (2)   (2)   (3)   (3)   (9)   (6)   (7)

NOTES FOR FURTHER REFLECTION

I have tried to keep the text of this book as lean as possible so that the reader can process the main thoughts without too many distractions. However, as I have read and thought about this subject, I have found much material that could supplement various points that I have made. Therefore, I offer these additional comments and quotes for those who would find them useful in exploring the subjects covered in this book.

The first two notes give concrete examples of how the presence and fear of Hell are real to many people even today.

1. While talking to a visitor at University Presbyterian Church about the book I was writing on Hell, the visitor said that he would write me a note telling me about an experience he had in the Assembly of God Church where his father was pastor in the mid-fifties. This is what he wrote:

   We had an ordained woman minister and friend of the family who did a series of "illustrated sermons" in our church on salvation. Fear was a big motivating factor in these sermons. One in the series was a depiction of Hell. She had a male adult in the church dressed in a devil outfit, complete with a red suit, tail, horns, and a pitchfork. There were also two or three elementary age children who played the parts of the devil's imps. With lights dimmed, on the platform of the sanctuary she had red and orange streamers blown by fans with lights to look like fire. She began her sermon about salvation and hell and at the appropriate time the devil and his imps would come out and pre-arranged individuals would be taken by them, screaming, and tossed into the fire as they begged for mercy. This was followed by the traditional call to repentance aimed at those who were not saved as well as backsliders. This was a time when few children had TV so the characters were more realistic to the children who were greatly frightened by the scene.

2. A colleague who recently came to be pastor to students and young adults at University Presbyterian, Ben Johnston Krase, recounted his first encounter with Hell in a sermon preached at our evening worship service.

> When I was in the second grade, my brother Ethan and I spent every school morning with our next door neighbor, Peggy Gowran. Our parents both worked in education and had to be out of the house long before we did. So, each morning we'd spend 45 minutes or so with Mrs. Gowran until it was time for us to walk to school. Mrs. Gowran did two things during that 45 minutes that we never did at home.

First, she did a Bible lesson with us and then, when the Bible lesson was over, she would give us a Pop Tart. Now I need to explain – we never ate those things at home, so this was always a real treat. In fact, at home we never even got sugar cereal, and so we would make those Pop Tarts last all the way to school if we could.

One morning, her Bible lesson was about Hell. Using a felt board she gave a fascinating presentation. When she was through, she turned to me and said, "Do you believe in Hell?"

I said, "I don't know."

She said, "Well, then, you don't get a Pop Tart."

Now, remember, I was in the second grade. Looking back, I wish I had said something like, "My theological convictions will not be bought with a Pop Tart!" But I didn't. You know, we're talking about the mind of a seven-year-old. And so, in the end, I said, "Ok, I believe in Hell," and she gave me the Pop Tart. Now I don't remember this to be a particularly traumatic moment in my childhood. But I haven't forgotten it, either.

3. Dennis Linn, Sheila Fabricant Linn, and Matthew Linn have written a wonderful book called *Good Goats*. The first section of the book is entitled, "Healing Our Image of God." In a chapter called "How My Image of God Changed," Matthew Linn tells about a woman named

Hilda who came to him distraught. Her son, a notorious sinner who wanted nothing to do with God, had tried for the fourth time to commit suicide. She wanted to know what would happen to her son in the life to come if he died without turning to God and repenting of his sins.

Matthew asked Hilda what she thought would happen to her son. She replied that because her son had lived such a bad life and had rejected God, she believed that God would certainly send him to Hell.

Matthew helped Hilda look at her question by asking her to close her eyes and imagine that she was sitting next to the judgment seat of God. She was also to imagine that her son had died an unrepentant sinner and had arrived at the judgment seat of God. When Hilda indicated that she had this image in her mind, Matthew asked her how her son felt as he stood there in that judgment scene. Hilda replied that her son felt lonely and empty. Matthew asked her what she wanted to do as she stood there observing this scene and Hilda said that she wanted to throw her arms around her son. She began to cry as she imagined herself holding her son tightly.

Then, Matthew asked Hilda to look into God's eyes and observe what God was doing. As she looked, God stepped down from the judgment throne, and just as Hilda had done, God embraced Hilda's son. And the three of them, Hilda, her son, and God, cried together and held each other tenderly.

4. The "Letters to the Editor" section of the *Austin American Statesman*, our local newspaper, printed an interesting letter on November 17, 2003. It speaks very forcefully

to the desire of laypeople to hear from theologians and preachers about the issues of exclusivity and inclusivity. The letter referred to a previous article written by Bill Young, which had suggested that respecting other faith traditions does not weaken our own beliefs. The writer of this letter agreed that we should all recognize that people are free to follow their faith traditions without interference.

But, then, the writer says (my emphasis in italics):

> However, Young's last paragraph regarding exclusiveness and inclusiveness of Christianity is most interesting. Isn't the conventional definition of Christianity the belief that Jesus of Nazareth (called the Christ) is the son of God, and access to God and his heaven is only through belief in Jesus' divinity and resurrection? If this is so, what then is Young's belief and ministry in this regard, and if otherwise than the conventional definition, is it appropriate to call his ministry "Christian"? *This exclusiveness/inclusiveness issue is of great concern to many thinking "lay" Christians, and we are eager for counsel from ministers and theologians.*

5. Perhaps the best way to talk about Heaven and Hell is by way of parables. In her book *My Grandfather's Blessing*, Rachel Naomi Remen tells a story that in many ways captures the essence of what I have tried to say about the true nature of what Heaven and Hell are all about. She says,

There is a parable about the difference between Heaven and Hell. In Hell people are seated at a table overflowing with delicious food. But they have splints on their elbows and so they cannot reach their mouths with their spoons. They sit through eternity experiencing a terrible hunger in the midst of abundance. In Heaven people are also seated at a table overflowing with delicious food. They, too, have splints on their elbows and cannot reach their mouths. But, in Heaven, people use their spoons to feed one another. Perhaps Hell is always of our own making. In the end, the difference between Heaven and Hell may only be that in Hell, people have forgotten how to bless one another. (p. 233)

6. In exploring the Roman Catholic Church's position on Hell, I found very helpful a book called *Idiot's Guide to Understanding Catholicism,* written by Bob O'Gorman and Mary Faulkner and published by Alpha Books in Indianapolis, Indiana. The authors say,

"Eternal damnation" is not attributed to an act of God, because in his merciful love, he can only desire our complete life with him. Hell is the pain produced by our choices of utterly and deliberately refusing to live in relationship with God, if such a choice is even possible. Hell is only a possibility because we take seriously the quality of free will God has created in us.

They go on to say,

> Speaking on the subject of Hell, Pope John Paul II said not to consider it a place, but rather a state that the soul suffers when it denies itself access to God. Hell is the ultimate consequence of sin. To describe this reality, scripture uses symbolic language. The images of hell that appear in sacred scripture must be properly interpreted, according to the Pope. They are used as an analogy to show the complete desperation and emptiness without God. Images of hell are a poetic warning. The Pope's remarks are directed at correcting the improper use of biblical images of hell that create anxiety and despair.

Finally, they add,

> The pope went on to say that God has never revealed "whether or which human beings" are eternally damned. As stated earlier, damnation is the result of a serious sin and requires that the person absolutely knows what he or she is doing. The church does not say this has ever happened to anyone. A good illustration occurs when Jesus does not condemn those who participated in his crucifixion. Rather, he says, "Father, forgive them, for they do not know what they are doing." (Luke 23:34) (pp. 272–273)

7. In his book *Eternal Life: Life After Death as a Medical, Philosophical, and Theological Problem*, Hans Küng quotes Catholic theologians Thomas and Gertrude Sartory who say in their book, *There is No Fire Burning in Hell*:

> No religion in the world (not a single one in the history of humanity) has on its conscience so many millions of people who thought differently, believed differently. Christianity is the most murderous religion there has ever been. Christians today have to live with this, they have to "overcome" this sort of past. And the real cause of this perversion of the Christian spirit is "belief in hell."

Küng concludes,

> If someone is convinced that God condemns a person to hell for all eternity for no other reason than because he is a heathen, a Jew or a heretic, he cannot for his own part fail to regard all heathens, Jews and heretics as good for nothing, as unfit to exist and unworthy of life. Seen from this standpoint, the almost complete extermination of the North and South American Indians by the "Christian" conquerors is quite consistent. (p. 132, *Eternal Life*)

8. This past October, during the Halloween season, I learned that a local Pentecostal Church was having what it called "Virtual Hell." On their website, I

found an article written for the Washington *Post* by Amanda Zamora. The headline read: "This Halloween, a church is scaring the hell out of the young."

Ms. Zamora went on to say, "With the help of some horror-flick scenery, high-tech machinery and willing young actors, an Austin Church has joined a tide of Christian ministries aiming to save their youth – by scaring them. Hundreds of teenagers are flocking to Virtual Hell, an extravagant haunted house with scripted scenes that the church says graphically depict the evils and consequences of abortion, homosexuality, suicide, domestic abuse and drugs. For $10.00 a teenager can spend Saturday night with the devil himself."

A friend and I decided to check out Virtual Hell. We went on a slow night and so the long lines we had been warned about did not materialize. As advertised, we were ushered by one of the devil's helpers along a path that led first to a car wreck scene replete with bleeding, dying teenagers strewn around, plus the requisite beer bottles that indicated that the wreck had been caused by a drunken driver. The next scene was a living room where a drinking husband was physically and verbally abusing his wife and daughter. In following scenes we saw a girl committing suicide, an abortion, a group of same-sex teenagers drinking and making out. The last part of the path lay over a bridge that shook as we walked across it with smoke rising from below. Here a very tall male dressed as the Devil accosted us. He asked each of us if we believed in Jesus with the very obvious implication that a "no" answer would mean that we were eternally damned.

Reflecting on what I had seen and heard, I concluded that this church had found a very dramatic way to get its message across that certain sins would lead to hellish consequences. However, several things troubled me – the narrow list of sins, the moralistic nature of all the sins, and the lack of any scenes depicting poverty or war or any other social sin.

Two things troubled me most. First, the lecture at the end of the tour of hell gave a very simplistic formula for avoiding these hells – namely, confess the name of Jesus and you will be able to avoid all these pitfalls. Secondly, the last scene conveyed the clear message to these young people that these sins on earth will lead to an eternal damnation. As the author of the *Post* article said in her headline, this church had found a way of scaring the hell out of these young people.

9. The November 29, 2003 edition of the *Austin American Statesman* contained an article entitled: "Number of 'Nones' who claim no religion swells." "Nones" are people who put "none" when asked on a questionnaire about their religious preference. Statistically, the nones grew from 8 percent of the U. S. population in 1990 to 14 percent in 2001. Nones are not necessarily atheist. Many nones believe in God but not in organized religion.

What particularly caught my attention in this article were the comments of a young woman named Leonard who explained why she left organized religion. According to this account,

Her doubts began at age 10 when she was told people who didn't attend Mass were barred from heaven. She immediately thought of "Pop," her beloved grandfather. "You're telling me that he's going to hell because he doesn't go to Mass on Sundays," she remembered asking.

Leonard, a publicist who works in New York City, came to see religion as "death insurance." She wasn't willing to pay the premiums. "I look at it and say, 'OK, I know I'm living the best life I can here and now,'" she said. "I just don't see the point of planning for something I don't know exists."

10. In an interview on beliefnet.com, Marcus Borg was asked, "How do you talk about a word like 'salvation' in this new paradigm?" His answer was,

In the Bible, salvation is mostly concerned with something that happens in this life. Even in the New Testament, the primary meaning of the word 'salvation' is transformation in this life. One can see this in the roots of the English word salvation, which comes from 'salve,' which is a healing ointment. Salvation is about healing. We all grow up wounded, and salvation is about the healing of the roots of existence.

Salvation is about light in darkness, liberation from bondage, return from exile, or reconnection with God. It is about hunger being satisfied, our thirst being quenched, and so forth. The identification of salvation with 'going to heaven' in much of popular

Christianity not only impoverishes the meaning of salvation but I also think really distorts what being a Christian is all about.

Borg concluded:

Whenever the afterlife is made central to being Christian, it invariably turns Christianity into a religion of requirements. And then suddenly Christianity ceases to be a religion of grace and instead becomes a religion of measuring up to what God requires. (http://www.beliefnet.com/story/135/story_13587.html)

ENDNOTES

Chapter 1

[1] Robert G. Ingersoll, *Ingersoll's Greatest Lectures* (New Jersey: Wehman Bros., 1940) p. 20

[2] Ingersoll, *Ingersoll's Greatest Lectures,* pp. 20–21

[3] Ingersoll, *Ingersoll's Greatest Lectures,* p. 22

[4] *Catechism of the Catholic Church* (Doubleday: New York, 1995) p. 292

Chapter 2

[5] Alice K. Turner, *The History of Hell* (New York: Harcourt Brace & Company, 1993) p. 1

[6] Alan E. Bernstein, *The Formation of Hell* (New York: Cornell University Press, 1995) p. 2

[7] Hans Küng, *Eternal Life? Life After Death as a Medical, Philosophical, and Theological Problem* (New York: Image Books) p. 141

Chapter 3

[8] James Carroll, *Constantine's Sword: The Church and the Jews* (Boston: Houghton Mifflin Company, 2001) p. 287

[9] Carroll, *Constantine's Sword,* pp. 288–289

[10] Rita Nakashima Brock, *Journeys By Heart* (New York: Crossroad, 1998) p. 56

[11] Walter Wink, *The Powers That Be* (New York: Galilee Doubleday, 1998) pp. 88–89

12. Shirley C. Guthrie, Jr., *Christian Doctrine* (Atlanta: John Knox Press, 1968) pp. 242–243.

13. Matthew Fox, *Original Blessing* (Santa Fe, New Mexico: Bear & Company, 1983) p. 47

14. Fox, *Original Blessing,* p. 47

15. Harold S. Kushner, *How Good Do We Have to Be? A New Understanding of Guilt and Forgiveness* (Boston: Little, Brown and Company, 1996) p. 21

16. Walter Brueggemann, *Genesis: Interpretation: A Bible Commentary for Teaching and Preaching* (Atlanta: John Knox Press, 1982) p. 41

17. Hans Küng, *On Being A Christian* (New York: Doubleday & Company, 1974) p. 315

18. Küng, *On Being A Christian,* p. 312

19. Norman Pittenger, *After Death Life in God* (New York: The Seabury Press, 1980) p. 10

20. Clara Sue Kidwell, Homer Noley, and George E. Tinker, *A Native American Theology* (New York: Orbis Books, 2001) p. 64

21. Kidwell et al, *A Native American Theology,* p. 65

Chapter 4

22. Nathaniel Micklem, *The Interpreter's Bible, Vol. II* (New York: Abingdon/Cokesbury, 1952) p. 12

23. Edith Hamilton, *Witness to the Truth* (New York: W.W. Norton & Company, 1948) p. 205

24. Robert Paul, *The Atonement and the Sacraments* (New York: Abingdon Press, 1960) pp. 50–51

25. Peter Berger, *The Heretical Imperative* (Garden City, New York; Anchor Press/Doubleday, 1980) p. 8

26. Don Browning, *Atonement and Psychotherapy* (Philadelphia: The Westminster Press, 1966) p. 246

27. Paul S. Fiddes, *Past Event and Present Salvation* (Louisville, Kentucky: Westminster/John Knox Press, 1989) p. 143

28. James Carroll, *Constantine's Sword* (Boston: Houghton Mifflin Company, 2001) pp. 293–294

29. David Everett Roberts, *Psychotherapy and a Christian View of Man* (New York: Charles Scribner's Sons, 1950) p. 33

30. Reuel L. Howe, *Man's Need and God's Action* (Greenwich, Connecticut: Seabury Press, 1953) pp. 88–89

31. Browning, *Atonement and Psychotherapy,* p. 183

32. Brock, *Journeys By Heart,* p. 7

33. Brock, *Journeys By Heart,* p. 7

34. Karen Armstrong, *Through the Narrow Gate* (New York: St. Martin's Press, 1981) p. 135

35. Armstrong, *Through the Narrow Gate,* p. 137

36. Rachel Naomi Remen, *My Grandfather's Blessings* (New York: Riverhead Books, 2000) p. 23

37. Remen, *My Grandfather's Blessings,* p. 23

Chapter 5

38. Marcus Borg, *Reading the Bible Again for the First Time* (HarperSanFrancisco, 2001) p. 255

39. M. Scott Peck, *The Road Less Traveled: A New Psychology of Love, Traditional Values and Spiritual Growth* (New York: A Touchstone Book, 1978) p. 15

40. C.S. Lewis, *The Great Divorce* (HarperSanFrancisco: 1946) p. 75

41. Lewis, *The Great Divorce,* p. 76–77

42. Lewis, *The Great Divorce,* p. 77

43. John Polkinghorne, *The God of Hope and the End of the World* (New Haven and London: Yale University Press, 2002) p. 137

Chapter 6

44. Gareth Lloyd Jones, *Journal of Beliefs & Values, Vol. 20, No. 2,* 1999

45. Polkinghorne, *The God of Hope and the End of the World,* p. 15

46. Polkinghorne, *The God of Hope and the End of the World,* p. 95

47. Polkinghorne, *The God of Hope and the End of the World,* p. 99

48. Mircea Eliade, *A History of Religious Ideas; Vol. I: From the Stone Age to the Eleusinian Mysteries* (University of Chicago Press, Chicago, 1979) pp. 9–10

49. Raymond A. Moody, *Life After Life* (St. Simons Island, Georgia: Mockingbird Books, 1975) p. 5

50. Küng, *Eternal Life,* p. 15

51. Küng, *Eternal Life,* p. 105

Chapter 7

[52.] Paul Woodruff and Harry A. Wilmer, editors, *Facing Evil* (LaSalle, Illinois: Open Court, 1988) p. 190

[53.] Walter Wink, *Engaging the Powers* (Minneapolis: Fortress Press, 1992) p. 6

[54.] Wink, *Engaging the Powers,* pp. 8–9

[55.] Wink, *Engaging the Powers,* p. 9

Chapter 8

[56.] Hans Küng, *Theology for the Third Millennium: An Ecumenical View* (New York: Doubleday, 1988) p. 227

[57.] Taken from a sermon preached on November 24, 2002, by the Reverend Dr. Frederick F. Ritsch, pastor of the Bethesda Presbyterian Church in Bethesda, Maryland.

INDEX

A

Abba **64**
Abelard **82, 83, 85, 86**
Abraham and Sarah **70**
acceptance **15, 83, 84, 86,
    104, 105**
Adam and Eve **52, 54, 59, 60,
    61, 63, 78, 132, 133, 137**
addiction **11, 14, 100, 106**
Agnostic **34**
Ahura Mazda **42**
Alcoholic Anonymous **106**
Amos **71**
Angra Mainyu **42**
Anselm **51, 53, 54, 55, 57, 59,
    61, 63, 64, 69, 82, 87, 89,
    102, 104**
Anubis **41**
Apostle Paul **80, 111, 148**
Armstrong, Karen **87**
atonement **36, 37, 54, 56, 57,
    66, 69, 80, 82**
Atonement and Psychotherapy **81**
Aulen, Gustav **80**
A Native American Theology **66**

B

Babylon **39, 45**
banquet **49, 50**
Bathsheba **72**
Beatitudes **124**
Berger, Peter **80**
Bernstein, Alan **46**
biblical references
    1 Corinthians 12:31 **148**
    1 Corinthians 13:1 **148**
    Acts 26:28 **53**
    Amos 4:1–3 **72**

Daniel 12:2–3 **46**
Deuteronomy 30:11–14 **63**
Deuteronomy 5:15 **70**
Exodus 34:6–7 **62**
Galatians 1:8 **31**
Genesis 2:16-17 **52**
Hebrews 2:14 **81**
Isaiah 14:9-15 **44**
Isaiah 34:8–10 **32**
Isaiah 53:5 **57**
Isaiah 66:24 **31**
Jeremiah 6:13–14 **95**
Jeremiah 31:33–34 **152**
Jeremiah 5:14 **95**
John 1:12 **53**
John 10:10 **47, 123**
John 12:31 **81**
John 3:16 **53**
Luke 10:27 **76**
Luke 16:19-31 **21, 28**
Luke 19:1–10 **107**
Luke 23:34 **110**
Luke 4:18,19 **47**
Luke 4:21 **47**
Mark 2:23–28 **77**
Mark 3:29 **32**
Matthew 23:23 **76**
Matthew 25:31-46 **28**
Matthew 25:31–46 **21**
Matthew 4:23 **124**
Matthew 5:22 **28**
Micah 6:8 **71**
Psalm 22:1 **135**
Psalm 88:3–7 **43**
Revelation 12:9 **81**
Revelation 20:15 **52**
Romans 5:12 **52**
Romans 5:8 **53**

Also by Keith Wright

Religious Abuse
A Pastor Explores the Many Ways
Religion Can Hurt as Well as Heal
Addresses a difficult and controversial topic.
ISBN 1-896836-47-X

If you enjoyed this book you may also enjoy these other books from Wood Lake Books and Northstone Publishing

Emmaus Road
Churches Making Their Way Forward
Donna Sinclair and Christopher White
Offers to readers what the first disciples experienced on the road to
Emmaus – an encounter with hope.
ISBN 1-55145-485-8

Jacob's Blessing
Dreams, Hopes, and Visions for the Church
Donna Sinclair and Christopher White
A hopeful and inspirational vision of the future of the church. Video and
study guide also available.
ISBN 1-55145-381-9

Dying Church, Living God
A Call to Begin Again
Chuck Meyer
Acknowledgement of the death of the church and the inevitable
resurrection is both the premise and the promise of this provocative,
enlightening book.
ISBN 1-896836-39-9

Future Faith Churches
Reconnecting with the Power of the Gospel for the 21st Century
Don Posterski & Gary Nelson
Churches showing the way into the next millennium.
ISBN 1-55145-098-4

There's Got to be More!
Connecting Churches and Canadians
Reginald Bibby
Explores how churches can reach new people.
ISBN 1-55145-048-8

Spiritscapes
Mapping the Spiritual and Scientific Terrain
at the Dawn of the New Millenium
Mark Parent
An overview and analysis of nine of the most significant spiritual and
scientific movements of our time.
ISBN 1-896836-11-9

Prayer
The Hidden Fire
Tom Harpur
Brings the broad theological perspective of prayer to the personal level.
ISBN 1-896836-40-2

Sin
A New Understanding of Virtue & Vice
James Taylor
Examines the fascinating origins and evolution of all seven deadly sins.
ISBN 1-896836-00-3

The Heart of Conflict
A Spirituality of Transformation
Dr. Elinor D.U. Powell
Brings spirituality into the realm of conflict and challenge.
ISBN 1-896836-57-7

Find these titles at any fine bookstore, or call 1.800.663.2775 for
more information. Check our website www.woodlakebooks.com

KEITH WRIGHT served as a pastor for 40 years in the Presbyterian Church USA. He received his Doctor of Ministry degree (1986) and the Distinguished Alumni Award (1992) from Austin Presbyterian Theological Seminary. Since his retirement in 1993, Dr. Wright has served as an interim associate pastor at Westminster Presbyterian Church, Covenant Presbyterian Church, and University Presbyterian Church in Austin, Texas. He is the author of *Religious Abuse: A Pastor Explores the Many Ways Religion Can Hurt as Well as Heal.*